TODAY'S GOURMET

Light and Healthy Cooking for the 1990s

JACQUES PÉPIN

BBC BOOKS

Published by BBC Books,
a division of BBC Enterprises Limited,
Woodlands, 80 Wood Lane
London W12 0TT.

First published in the UK 1993

ISBN 0 563 36947 7

Designed by Casbourne Rose Design Associates
Set in Sabon by Goodfellow and Egan Ltd, Cambridge
Printed and bound in Great Britain by Redwood Books, Ltd, Trowbridge
Cover printed by Clays Ltd, St Ives Plc

Contents

THE production of *Today's Gourmet*, the television series as well as the cookbook, required a concerted effort on the part of many, many capable people, and I would like to thank everyone involved with these projects for their support and hard work. It is impossible to name every person associated with all the various facets of the programme and book, but the people I especially want to thank are:

Marjorie Poore, my executive producer at KQED, for her indefatigable drive to find sponsorship for the show, and the confidence this reflected in me; Peter Stein, my producer, for his vision and cooperation; Linda Brandt, my associate producer, who worked diligently on both the series and the book; Katherine Russell, my capable director; Susie Heller, my culinary advisor and dear friend, for her enthusiasm and hard work; Bernie Schimbke, who ably directed set and food styling; Ken Short, for his outstanding set designs; and of course, Dan Bowe, my great back kitchen supervisor, and his wonderful staff: Travis Brady, Jeff Forman, Robin Margolin, Amy McKenzie, and Michael Pollock.

JACQUES PÉPIN

This book was originally written for American readers and, therefore, includes American cup measurements. The following conversion charts show the metric and imperial equivalents of cup measurements. As the conversions are only approximate, please follow one set of measurements only. Readers may find it useful to buy a set of American cup measures.

DRY INGREDIENTS

American	Metric	Imperial
1/4 cup	50 g	2 oz
1/2 cup	100 g	4 oz
3/4 cup	175 g	6 oz
1 cup	225 g	8 oz

LIQUID INGREDIENTS

American	Metric	Imperial
1/4 cup	50 m	2 fl oz
1/2 cup	100 m	4 fl oz
3/4 cup	175 m	6 fl oz
1 cup	225 m	8 fl oz

Introduction

'This is a sensitive and sensible way to cook, a cooking style that emphasizes aspects of health in a common-sense way ... yet still exhibits elegance and joy in its creation.'

When I recall the food that we used to serve at *Le Pavillon* in New York thirty years ago when I first came to the United States, I realise how much cooking in general has changed and improved especially in the last twenty years or so.

I like to think that my cooking has changed a great deal, too. Through the years, I have tried to keep abreast of what's going on and have made adjustments in my cooking to accommodate such changes as those brought about by the social upheavals of the 1960s and 1970s, spanning everything from women's liberation to organic gardening – one offshoot of a tremendous worldwide concern about health.

Paradoxically, it is interesting to note that the current preoccupation with health as it relates to food is not a new or revolutionary phenomenon. Dating back as far as the ancient Greek poet and gastronome Archestratus, and the Romans, and continuing on through the cooking of the sixteenth, seventeenth and eighteenth centuries, food has always been closely associated with health.

In fact, most cookbooks prior to the nineteenth century were gastro-medical in nature, and there are early twentieth-century examples of these as well: a book by Dr Edouard de Pomaine, published during the Second World War, dealt with healthy eating in times when food supplies were scarce.

The trend today is a return to that basic notion of health encapsulated in Brillat-Savarin's aphorism stating 'you are what you eat'. The same notion was expressed later by Thomas Alva Edison, who said, 'The doctor of the future will give no medicine, but will educate his patients in the care of the human frame, in diet, and in the cause and prevention of disease'.

'The concerns of modern, well-educated eaters parallel those of modern, well-educated young chefs and go beyond how food tastes and how it is presented ... The quality of the products in our diet directly affects the quality of our health and the health of our families.'

The concerns of modern, well-educated eaters parallel those of modern, well-educated young chefs and go beyond how food tastes and how it is presented. Today's astute food buyer wants produce that is not only fresh, but is free of chemicals. The quality of the products in our diet directly affects the quality of our health and the health of our families. We have to stay in tune with nature; if the chickens we eat feed on grass and natural grains in an area free of pesticides and insecticides, their quality and the quality of the eggs they produce will be substantially better.

Health concerns me greatly in *Today's Gourmet*. Although this is not intended to be a low-calorie, low-fat, low-sodium or low-cholesterol cookbook, the recipes here reflect how important I think it is to moderate these nutritional components. Keep in mind, however, that I am a cook, not a doctor. I am not a guru of macrobiotic food, insisting on wholesome grains and fibre, nor have I assumed the role of a nutritionist, advising people what they should or should not eat. Eating, for me, has always meant enjoyment and sharing, never obligation.

On these pages, I want to introduce you to a cuisine that demonstrates a rational approach to cooking. This is a sensitive and sensible way to cook, a cooking style that emphasises aspects of health in a common-sense way – a diverse diet with more fibre and less saturated fat, more fish and shellfish, smaller portions of well-trimmed meat, vegetables cooked in a manner that preserves vitamins and nutrients – yet still exhibits elegance and joy in its creation. This is the cuisine of today and the cuisine of tomorrow, and it represents a lower-calorie, healthier, faster and simpler way of cooking.

In a true reflection of life, some of the recipes are more concerned with health than others. When we join with friends and family on holidays and special occasions, we sometimes don't count calories – we indulge. At other times, we are more careful. I still use butter, salt, and cream, although parsimoniously, adding them in small amounts at the moment when they most influence taste. Essentially, this is modern cooking – a blend of substance and sophistication, contemporary food that appeals to everyone.

This kind of cooking avoids gimmicks and trends, rather satisfies the tastes of a more discriminating audience while meeting their nutritional needs in a non-prescriptive way. I want a cuisine that appeals to the epicurean and the sports enthusiast as well as the home cook and the single professional. I even make suggestions for people on special diets on how they can adapt my recipes to satisfy their personal requirements.

As a professional chef, I also want to teach proper cooking techniques by demonstrating how these techniques can save time and effort and so make cooking that much more enjoyable. My cuisine is not a complicated or contrived mix of esoteric ingredients, and it is not intended for an elitist group of people. It is for everyone. Everyone should know how to defat a stock, how to trim a piece of meat properly, and how to prepare beef, pork, and other foods not usually associated with lighter cuisine in a healthy way.

Finally, I want to show the importance of togetherness, convivality and *joie de vivre* in the kitchen. Cooking should be exciting – nothing compares to the enjoyment of sharing good food while spending time with family and friends. But most of all, I hope that the knowledge readers gain from *Today's Gourmet* will make their lives richer, healthier, and happier.

Menus

On the following pages I have listed the twenty-six different menus that are featured in my television series, Today's Gourmet. *Any sort of recipe grouping is arbitrary, however, influenced by such factors as market considerations and personal food preferences.*

Use my listings merely as a point of departure. Reorganise as you wish, extrapolating a recipe from one menu and adding it to another.

Although there aren't any salad recipes in the book, you'll note that I have listed them on most of my menus. We eat salads every day, and I recommend them for taste and because they help balance a diet. Bread and wine are also part of our daily fare. If you include them with your meals as well, remember to take into account the added calories.

Although we don't have dessert on a daily basis at home, preferring to end our meal with fresh fruit, I have included dessert recipes here to complete the menus and make them special enough to serve when you entertain.

MY MOTHER'S FAVOURITES

THIS menu reminds me of home. The garlic soup, containing potatoes and leeks, and the roast of veal, cooked in a Dutch oven with artichokes and lots of garlic, reminds me of my youth in France. The almond cake dessert, originally called *pain de Gênes* or 'bread of Genoa', is usually very rich, calling for lots of egg yolks and butter. But in my version, I have reduced the number of calories in the cake and substituted a mango coulis with plenty of flavour for the traditional rich custard sauce.

Garlic Soup

Veal Roast with Artichokes

Salad

Almond Cake with Mango Coulis

MEDITERRANEAN FLAVOURS

IN this menu, I have tried to capture the diverse flavours of the Mediterranean region. I begin with tuna tartare served on a bed of marinated cucumbers, which suggests regions of Italy or the South of France. Next comes a classic dish – in fact one might call it the national dish of Spain – paella. Saffron-flavoured rice is combined with pieces of hot sausage, chicken, an assortment of shellfish and of course, fresh vegetables. For dessert, I have chosen figs poached in a spicy port sauce. It reminds me of Portugal with a touch of Italy thrown in, because after all, I do use Campari in the sauce.

Tuna Tartare on Marinated Cucumbers

Chicken and Seafood Paella

Salad

Figs in Spicy Port Sauce

NOUVELLE CUISINE

THIS menu features robust, lusty dishes characteristic of nouvelle cuisine – very fresh ingredients, quickly cooked light sauces and interesting combinations of food with great eye appeal. In the first course, the potato crêpe is thicker than a conventional one, more like a pancake, and it is garnished with two different types of caviar, sour cream and herbs. Grilled chicken breast, without its skin and thinly sliced, is served on a bed of shredded cabbage seasoned with anchovies, garlic and olive oil. I finish the menu with a deliciously light chocolate cake served with a concentrated raspberry-rum sauce.

Potato Crêpes with Caviar

Grilled Chicken with Cabbage Anchoïade

Salad

Chocolate Soufflé Cake with Raspberry-Rum Sauce

A PARTY MENU

THIS type of menu makes life easier when you invite a group of friends over for a casual party. The braised leeks with tomatoes are best served at room temperature so they are perfect in a buffet setting. This is true, too, of the smoked pork shoulder roast with mustard-honey glaze. I place it on the buffet table along with a sharp knife and let guests help themselves. A bowl of braised cabbage is set out as an accompaniment, as well as a simple salad. And for dessert, strawberry shortcake is always a hit. You can assemble it in advance or bring everything to the table and let guests serve themselves.

Leeks with Tomato and Olive Oil

Smoked Pork Roast with Mustard-Honey Glaze

Braised Sour Cabbage

Salad

Buttermilk Strawberry Shortcakes

COOKING AGAINST THE CLOCK

IF you cook in the following sequence, this interesting menu can be ready in half an hour. Begin by making the bulgar. While it cooks, prepare the pineapple and let it macerate in the liqueur. Then grill the lamb chops and as they cook, begin the first course by sautéing the damp greens. Arrange them on plates. Next remove the cooked lamb and let it rest in a warm oven. Then sauté the prawns and arrange over the greens. Finish the bulgar and prepare the tomato salad. Finally, finish and serve the lamb chops and complete the pineapple dessert.

Hot Prawns on Spinach

Grilled Lamb Chops with Savory

Curried Bulgar with Currants

Tomato, Onion and Parsley Vinaigrette

Salpicon of Pineapple

EARTHY COUNTRY COOKING

THIS hearty menu begins with a gratin of spring onions. Although made with full-fat milk, it is still relatively low in fat. The same is true with the delicious ragout of rabbit. Another grain to give variety to your repertoire of complex carbohydrates is cornmeal (or maize flour) and this version, flavoured with Gruyère, is no exception. A salad is next, followed by a fresh fruit fondue with a delightful apricot dipping sauce.

Gratin of Spring Onions

Ragout of Rabbit

Cornmeal au Gruyère

Salad

Fresh Fruit with Minted Apricot Fondue

BISTRO COOKING OF NEW YORK

ALTHOUGH slightly more trendy than most French bistro food, New York bistro food is somewhat similar. Young chefs everywhere – and especially in New York – are interested in a lighter, more imaginative cuisine, one that will satisfy not only the epicurean, but the average person who wants to eat flavourful food without feeling guilty. The aubergine rolls contain many different vegetables combined with fresh, spicy seasonings. Cooked between layers of sliced potato, the red snapper remains moist and crisp. Following a salad, I finish with my interpretation of a classic bistro dish, apple tart.

Sautéed Aubergine Rolls

Red Snapper in Potato Jackets

Salad

Baked Apple Tart

A HEARTY SUPPER

THIS is a meal to come home to on a cold night! Begin with clam croquettes, followed by a favourite of mine, meat and vegetables that have been braised together until all their juices blend. To the well-trimmed pork, I add dried tomatoes, onions, garlic and carrots, all of which lend an appealing flavour to the cooking juices. The courgette-sauced pasta complements the main course. Next comes a salad, followed by the perfect conclusion, caramelized apple timbales.

Clam Croquettes

Braised Pork Cocotte

Pasta with Courgette Sauce

Salad

Caramelized Apple Timbales

THE HEALTHY GOURMET

HERE is a menu that concentrates on lowering calories. In fact, the total calorie count for the entire meal is about 700 calories per person, with less than 22 per cent of these coming from fat. Braised with lemon juice, the steamed chicory is a refreshing first course selection. Poached chicken is served with an assortment of vegetables, and the concentrated broth, with croûtons. After a salad, I offer a dessert – a large, cone-shaped biscuit filled with grapes and dried currants or raisins.

Steamed Chicory in Lemon Juice

Chicken Consommé with Croûtons

Poule au Pot

Salad

Grapes and Raisins in Lime Biscuit Cones

POT POURRI DINNER

THIS menu is interesting because it combines a new style of dishes that have become popular in the last few years. *Beef Carpaccio*, a re-interpretation of steak tartare, is great to serve for supper or an after-the-theatre party. You can make it ahead and it is always well received. Delicious fresh trout, served on a bed of fibre-rich ratatouille, is a very satisfying main course followed by a simple salad of mixed greens. And then comes dessert – a wonderful hazelnut parfait.

Beef Carpaccio

Trout on Ratatouille

Salad

Hazelnut Parfait with Candied Violets

HOLIDAY TRADITIONS

WE splurge a little over the holidays and expand our menu, but even so, at 1200 calories per serving, this meal is conservative compared to most holiday fare. Garnished with mangetouts and red pepper, the first-course scallop dish is colourful and original. Oven-roasted turkey contains a mushroom stuffing made with wholewheat bread and the ginger-flavoured carrot purée makes a delightful accompaniment. Our double holiday dessert – *Chocolate Mint Truffles* and *Candied Orange Rind* – offers a festive finish to this holiday menu.

Sautéed Scallops with Mangetouts

Roasted Turkey with Mushroom Stuffing

Carrot Purée with Ginger

Salad

Chocolate Mint Truffles

Candied Orange Rind

BIG TASTE ON A SMALL BUDGET

HERE is a menu that emphasises economy in the kitchen. I love to make vegetable soup and finish it with pasta such as vermicelli. It takes only a few minutes and is a great way to use leftover vegetables – something that I always have in my refrigerator. The main course consists of lean sausage meat wrapped in cabbage leaves, grilled and then served on a bed of lentils. And for the finale, try this delicious fruit dessert that combines baked pears and figs.

Potage de Légumes au Vermicelli

Saucisses au Chou on Le. tils

Salad

Baked Pears with Figs

COOKING FOR THE FAMILY

BECAUSE much of this meal can be prepared ahead, including the colourful chocolate cups filled with nuts and bits of fruit, it is a great menu to cook with the family at weekends. Kids love to help make potato pancakes. These are filled with a tasty mushroom mixture. The main course, veal chops served with a simple corn and red pepper sauté, is always a hit. And don't forget to include the family when making dessert. Pieces of fresh and dried fruit, nuts and seeds are pressed into small cups of melted chocolate. When they harden, peel off the paper wrappers and serve.

Mushroom-stuffed Potato Pancakes

Veal Chops with Mushrooms

Corn and Pepper Sauté

Salad

Chocolate and Fruit Nut Cups

SPRING ELEGANCE

CELEBRATE spring with this elegant, well-balanced menu. All the vegetables – peas, carrots, asparagus – plus the fresh strawberries served in a deliciously light 'floating island' dessert, provide a wonderful source of fibre, complex carbohydrates and vitamins. Even the beef roast meets the recommended daily allowance of no more than one-third of our calorie intake coming from fat.

Asparagus in Mustard Sauce

Spicy Beef Roast

Carotte Ciboulette

Peas à la Francaise

Pistachio Floating Island with Blackcurrant Sauce

COOKING FOR FRIENDS

COOKING for friends is a great pleasure for me and here is one of my favourite menus. I begin by serving steamed cod on tapenade, followed by *Poulet au Vin Rouge*. The classic chicken dish is garnished with mushrooms, glazed shallots and croûtons, and is served with a garlic-flavoured potato and turnip mixture. To conclude, I serve fresh blueberries topped with plain yoghurt and a sprinkling of brown sugar. The brown sugar melts through the yoghurt, creating a nice design.

Steamed Cod on Tapenade

Poulet au Vin Rouge

Turnips and Mashed Potatoes

Salad

Blueberries with Brown Sugar

COUNTRY FRENCH/BELGIAN MENU

COMBINING mussels and fried potatoes is actually Belgian in derivation but my 'French' family really enjoys this combination, too. Where I live, mussels are plentiful and inexpensive in the summertime, so when temperatures soar, we prefer to cook both the mussels and the french fries outdoors. Another family favourite, braised stuffed artichokes, is a nice accompaniment. For dessert, we all enjoy a light version of traditional coffee crème caramel.

Braised Stuffed Artichokes

Moules Maison

French Fries

Salad

Coffee Crème Caramel

CASUAL AND SIMPLE

AN interesting composite of different tastes, textures and colours highlights this delicious menu. For starters, fresh vegetable sauce over pasta is a healthy, high-fibre alternative to more common pasta sauces made with butter and cream. Next, I like to marinate well-trimmed leg of lamb in a pungent sauce, then grill it and serve with a spring onion and cauliflower dish. And for dessert, I make a cherry bread pudding, assembled and baked in a gratin dish and flavoured with almonds.

Pasta with Fresh Vegetable Sauce

Grilled Leg of Lamb

Cauliflower in Spring Onion Sauce

Salad

Cherry Bread Pudding

A SAVOURY BREAKFAST

IN this menu, you will find many different recipes, some with variations. Although I have provided more than you would want to serve for any one breakfast or brunch, the menu gives you an idea of what can be prepared for a savoury type of breakfast, rather than one containing an abundance of sweets. There are three variations of the basic *Oeuf Cocotte*, a smoked salmon mould, tasty oatmeal-leek soup, a classic mushroom omelette, hearty buttermilk bread and a fruit dish combining grapefruit and orange segments.

Oeuf Cocotte

Smoked Salmon Mould

Oatmeal Leek Soup

Mushroom Omelette

Orange and Grapefruit Segments

LIGHT AND LEISURELY

THIS elegant menu emphasises speed in the kitchen, speed that is based, at least most of the time, on a thorough understanding of the dishes you are about to prepare. The first course contrasts pink-coloured salmon against the green of fresh spinach and makes for a beautiful presentation. And what a great mixture of vegetables in the chicken dish, from mushrooms and garlic to shallots and yams. After the salad comes a simple ending to this well-balanced meal – a baked banana dessert served with a zesty lemon sauce.

Sautéed Salmon on Greens

Chicken Legs with Wine and Yams

Salad

Baked Bananas in Lemon-Rum Sauce

GREAT SANDWICHES

A MENU of great-tasting sandwiches can be varied ad infinitum. Sandwiches are a great way to use cold or leftover meats, fish or even vegetables. They can be complex as in a *Pan Bagna*, with many vegetables, or simple as *James Beard's Onion Sandwiches*. And they are versatile – serve them with any meal, as well as on picnics or buffets. Good cooks know that the most essential component of any sandwich is the bread. This high-gluten bread, which can easily be made in the food processor, is wonderfully adaptable and, depending on the grain and flour you use, the variations are endless.

Rolls and Baguettes

Roasted Aubergine Sandwiches

Olive and Tomato Toasts

James Beard's Onion Sandwiches

Pan Bagna

Smoked Salmon and Cucumber Sandwiches

Jam 'Sandwiches'

CLASSIC AND CHIC

THE food in this menu is delicious as well as beautiful to look at. Don't be afraid to use unusual ingredients such as sunflower seeds or quinoa, a delightful grain that is very high in protein. Although quail and fresh trout may sound a bit esoteric, you will be surprised at how easy they are to prepare with terrific results. Following the salad, the menu ends with a raspberry granité, a concentrated sherbet made with raspberry purée. It provides the perfect finish to this meal.

Trout Sauté Terry

Grilled Quail

Quinoa with Sunflower Seeds

Salad

Raspberry Granité

BISTRO COOKING OF LYON

BISTRO cooking implies casualness and sophistication at the same time. The setting is usually simple, while the food – although comfortable, recognisable and familiar – is slightly more sophisticated than you would prepare at home. I think that those little unpretentious restaurants called *bistros* in Lyon serve the most authentic French cooking you can find in France. For the first course, I combine beans with broccoli. With the main steak dish, I serve sautéed potatoes, followed by a salad. I finish with a refreshing baked apricot dessert.

Beans and Escarole

Wine Merchant Steak

Pommes Persillade

Salad

Baked Apricots with Almonds

AROUND-THE-WORLD MENU

THIS menu is diverse, composed of dishes from around the world that work well together. The crabmeat cakes come from the southern United States, although I've given them an unusual twist with the addition of avocado sauces. Irish lamb stew is a classic. Made from either lamb shoulder or leg of lamb, it includes a wide assortment of simmering vegetables. Following a salad, I like to serve an interesting dessert of dried figs studded with fresh almonds, similar to those found in the markets of southern Portugal.

Crab Cakes with Avocado Sauce

Irish Lamb Stew

Salad

Figs Villamora

LOW-CAL STEAMED DINNER

WEIGHT-WATCHERS will like this special menu because it contains fewer than 600 calories per serving and less than 26 per cent of that total is from fat. And everything cooks together in about a half an hour. You can prepare the salmon and the two side dishes in a three-tiered steamer, staggering the cooking times. I begin steaming the potatoes. After they have cooked for about 15 minutes, I start the broccoli. Finally, after the vegetables have cooked for a while longer, I steam the salmon. There is even time to assemble two sauces – one for the salmon and one for the broccoli – and make dessert.

Salmon Pojarski

Pommes Anglaises

Broccoli Piquante

Salad

Oranges in Grand Marnier

THE THRIFTY KITCHEN

THE dishes featured here would not be served together. Instead, this 'menu' exemplifies the concept of economy in the kitchen, demonstrating what can be done with different parts of a chicken. Three of the recipes are made with chicken parts that you might ordinarily discard – the skin, the carcass and the gizzard. Perhaps the most sophisticated dish on the menu, chicken served in a tarragon-flavoured sauce, is made with the breast and leg meat, which is poached in white wine and finished with a tarragon cream. Interestingly enough, this dish has fewer calories than any of the others because it is poached in wine rather than sautéed in fat. And the amount of cream added is negligible, amounting to only 1 tablespoon, or 45 calories per person.

Split Pea Soup with Crackling

Brown Rice Chicken Fricassee

Chicken in Tarragon Sauce

Salad

Fruit Medley

NEW ENGLAND SUMMER SUPPER

IN the summer along the coast of Connecticut we eat a lot of lobster, usually steaming it and serving it with corn on the cob and potatoes. Sometimes, however, I like to incorporate lobster into a more elegant menu. In this recipe lobster is made with couscous, a quick-cooking granulated wheat that cooks up fluffy and tender. Instead of a calorific butter sauce, I serve it with a delicate chive sauce made from the reduced cooking stock, a little olive oil and minced chives. The smooth chicken and spinach-flavoured *velouté* makes a satisfying first course and for dessert, we have individual *Crêpes Soufflés* served with a tangy grapefruit sauce.

Chicken and Spinach Velouté

Couscous of Lobster

Salad

Crêpes Soufflés in Grapefruit Sauce

The First Course

Garlic Soup
Chicken and Spinach Velouté
Potage de Légumes au Vermicelli
Split Pea Soup with Crackling
Chicken Broth
Oatmeal Leek Soup
Braised Stuffed Artichokes
Asparagus in Mustard Sauce
Beans and Escarole
Leeks with Tomato and Olive Oil
Steamed Endive in Lemon Juice
Sautéed Aubergine Rolls
Gratin of Spring Onions
Pasta with Courgettes
Pasta with Fresh Vegetable Sauce
Mushroom-stuffed Potato Pancakes
Potato Crêpes with Caviar
Crab Cakes with Avocado Sauce
Clam Croquettes
Smoked Salmon Mould
Steamed Cod on Tapenade
Sautéed Salmon on Greens
Tuna Tartare on Marinated Cucumbers
Trout Sauté Terry
Sautéed Scallops with Mangetouts
Hot Prawns on Spinach
Mussels Gratinée
Beef Carpaccio

Garlic Soup

ALONG with some leek and onion, there is a lot of garlic in this soup. Cooked here in liquid, however, its flavour is quite subtle, even mild. As a thickening agent, I use potato, although the same soup can be thickened with leftover bread, couscous or cornmeal instead. My mother used to finish this soup with cream, but I use milk; the result is wonderfully satisfying.

SERVES 4

1 leek, about 100 g (4 oz)
1 onion, about 100 g (4 oz)
2 tablespoons groundnut oil
8 cloves garlic, peeled and crushed (about 2 tbsp)
2 cups unsalted chicken stock, preferably homemade (see Chicken Broth, page 31)
2 cups water
450 g (1 lb) potatoes, peeled and cut into 2-inch chunks
1 teaspoon salt
1/2 teaspoon freshly ground black pepper
2 slices white bread
1 tablespoon corn oil
1 cup milk

1 Pre-heat the oven to gas mark 6, 400°F (200°C).

2 Trim the leek, wash it well, and cut it into 2.5 cm (1 in) pieces. (You should have about 1 cup.) Peel and coarsely chop the onion.

3 Heat the groundnut oil in a saucepan and when hot, add the leeks, onions and garlic, and sauté for 2 minutes. Then add the stock, water, potatoes, salt and pepper, and bring to a boil. Cover, reduce the heat to low, and boil gently for 25 minutes.

4 Meanwhile remove the crusts from the bread and cut it into 1 cm (1/2-in) croûtons. (You should have 1 1/4 cups.) Moisten the croûtons with the vegetable oil and spread them on a baking sheet. Place in the preheated oven for 8 to 10 minutes, until nicely browned.

5 When the soup is cooked, strain it through a sieve, retaining the liquid. Place the solids in the bowl of a food processor and process until smooth. Return to the saucepan with the reserved liquid and add the milk. Bring to a boil and serve with the croûtons.

Chicken and Spinach Velouté

THE quality of this soup depends on the quality of the chicken stock used. Home-made chicken stock shoul dbe completely defatted and highly concentrated. Although I thicken it with Cream of Wheat, which cooks quite quickly, you can use tapioca or semolina, any of which would work equally well.

SERVES 4

4 cups unsalted chicken stock, preferably homemade (see Chicken Broth, page 31)

1 cup water

3/4 teaspoon salt

1/4 teaspoon freshly ground black pepper

6 tablespoons instant Cream of Wheat, or tapioca or semolina

175 g (6 oz) spinach, stems removed and washed

1/3 cup double cream

1 Bring the stock, water, salt and pepper to a boil in a stainless steel saucepan. Add the Cream of Wheat, tapioca or semolina, mix well, bring back to the boil, and cook gently for 3 minutes.

2 Cut the washed spinach very coarsely and add it to the pan. Bring back to the boil and boil for 2 minutes. Stir in the cream and serve immediately.

Potage de Légumes au Vermicelli

ALTHOUGH I serve this hearty soup as a first course, it would also make a satisfying light supper on its own with the additon of a crunchy bread, a salad and a piece of cheese to finish the meal.

SERVES 6

1 tablespoon virgin olive oil

1/2 tablespoon unsalted butter

1 leek, about 750 g (3 oz), trimmed of damaged leaves, cleaned, and cut into 1 cm (1/2 in) pieces

1 medium onion, about 100 g (4 oz), peeled and coarsely chopped

2 carrots, about 100 g (4 oz), peeled and cut into 1 cm (1/2 in) pieces

1 courgette, about 100 g (4 oz), trimmed and cut into 2 cm (3/4 in) pieces

4 mushrooms, 100 g (4 oz), coarsely chopped

1 yam, about 175 g (6 oz), peeled and cut into 1 cm (1/2 in) pieces

7 cups water

1 teaspoon salt

1/4 teaspoon freshly ground black pepper

1 cup vermicelli, angel-hair pasta or very thin noodles, about 20 g (3/4 oz)

1 Heat the oil and butter in a saucepan. When hot, add the leeks and onions and sauté for 2 minutes. Then add the carrots, courgette, mushrooms and yams and mix well. Add the water, salt and pepper.

2 Bring to a boil, cover, reduce and heat and boil gently for about 12 mintues.

3 Add the pasta, bring back to the boil and cook, covered for about 4 minutes. Serve.

MAKING SOUP

My choice of vegetables for this soup is based on what is available in my refrigerator. In addition, while I thicken the soup here with vermicelli (angel-hair pasta), you could use another type of starch – from oatmeal to couscous or tapioca.

Split Pea Soup with Crackling

SPLIT peas are extremely high in soluble fibre. This is a great winter recipe when served with crusty bread and a simple first-course salad. The soup can be frozen, although it might require additional water when reheated, since it tends to thicken.

SERVES 6

175 g (6 oz) chicken skin cut into 2.5 cm (1 in) pieces

2 medium onions, about 226 g (8 oz), peeled and cut into 2.5 cm (1 in) pieces

2-3 cloves garlic, peeled, crushed and coarsely chopped

8 cups water

2 teaspoons herbes de Provence

2 teaspoons salt

1/2 teaspooon freshly ground black pepper

1/4 teaspoon Tabasco sauce

450 g (1 lb) dry split peas

1 Place the chicken skin pieces in a frying pan and sauté over high heat for 8 to 10 minutes, until the fat is rendered and the skin is crisp. Remove the crackling and fat and discard all but 3 tablespoons of the fat.

2 Place the reserved fat and crackling in a large saucepan, add the onion, and sauté for 5 minutes. Then add the garlic, mix well, and stir in the water, *herbes de Provence*, salt, pepper, Tabasco sauce and split peas.

3 Bring to a boil, cover, reduce the heat and boil gently for 1 hour. Stir the soup well; although it should be fairly thick, if you would prefer it thinned a little, add some water.

4 To serve, divide the soup among six bowls, and offer extra Tabasco sauce, if desired.

MAKING CRACKLING

For the crackling, I cook the chicken skin until it renders its fat and becomes crisp. I discard most of the cooking fat, retaining only 3 tablespoons, which I use to brown the onions for the soup. If you want to reduce your calorie intake further, eliminate the crackling altogether and just use the chicken fat or 3 tablespoons of peanut oil to start your soup.

Chicken Broth

THERE is nothing like the smell of a stock slowly cooking on the stove. Fresh stock is easy to make, inexpensive, and far better than any store-bought version. It does require a little time, but the amount of work involved is minimal. Take advantage of a day at home to make stock; you can be doing other things while it cooks, and then you can strain, package, and freeze it for use when needed. It is well worth the time and effort.

MAKES 2.25 LITRES (4 PINTS)

1.5 kg (3lb) chicken bones and necks
5.5 litres (10 pints) water
2 shallots
1 piece of ginger, about the size of a large shallot
1 star anise
1 tablespoon herbes de Provence

1 Place the bones and water in a heavy-based saucepan and bring to a boil over high heat. Reduce the heat, and simmer for 15 minutes. Skim off and discard the fat and impurities.

2 Impale the shallots and ginger on a skewer and hold over a flame (or place under a grill) for 4 to 5 minutes, turning occasionally, until black on all sides. Add to the stock to impart taste and colour. Stir in the star anise and *herbes de Provence*, and boil gently for 2 hours, partially covered.

3 Strain, cool, and remove all fat from the surface as directed. Refrigerate or freeze.

A WORD ABOUT STRAINING
The stock may be strained through kitchen paper to eliminate as much fat as possible. If time permits, it is a good idea to chill the stock until the fat solidifies on top. After it hardens, you can remove and discard this additional fat with ease.

Oatmeal Leek Soup

THIS soup can be prepared in a few minutes. I use whole milk, but you can use skimmed milk or something in-between if it meets your calorie needs better. You can substitute spring onions for the leeks, too, and use cornmeal to thicken the soup instead of oats.

SERVES 4

1 small leek
3½ cups whole milk
¼ teaspoon freshly ground black pepper
½ teaspoon salt
1 cup quick-cooking oats

1 Trim the leek, wash it well and chop finely, to make about 1 cup.

2 In a saucepan, bring the leek, milk, pepper and salt to a boil. Simmer for 2 minutes and then stir in the oats.

3 Cook for a further 2 minutes. Serve immediately, or keep warm in a double boiler over warm water.

Note: If the soup thickens, thin to desired consistency with milk or water.

Braised Stuffed Artichokes

INSTEAD of stuffing these artichokes, you can serve them simply with a little olive oil and lemon juice. If you do this, however, increase the initial cooking time from 20 to 30 minutes for this size of artichoke, since they won't be cooked additionally as the stuffed ones are.

SERVES 4

4 large artichokes, about 225 g (8 oz) each

6 tablespoons virgin olive oil

2 medium onions, about 175 g (6 oz), peeled and chopped

3 cloves garlic, peeled, crushed, and chopped (1½ tsp)

175 g (6 oz) mushrooms, rinsed and coarsely chopped

3 slices white bread

¾ teaspoon salt

¾ teaspoon freshly ground black pepper

1 cup water

1 Prepare the artichokes as described below.

For stuffing:

1 Heat 4 tablespoons of the olive oil in a frying pan and sauté the onions in the hot oil for about 1 minute. Add the garlic and mushrooms, and continue sautéeing for about 2 minutes.

2 Tear the bread slices into the bowl of a food processor and process for a few seconds, until crumbed. You should have about 1½ cups of crumbs. Add the breadcrumbs to the mixture in the pan and sauté for about 3 to 4 minutes, until nicely browned. Stir in ½ teaspoon each of the salt and pepper, and set aside.

3 When the artichokes are cool enough to handle, hold them upside down over the sink and squeeze out as much water as possible. Remove the thin

PERFECT ARTICHOKES

With a large, sharp knife, trim about 4 cm (1½ in) from the tops of the artichokes. Using scissors, cut off the thorny top third of the remaining leaves. Bring about 6 cups of water to the boil in a saucepan. Add the artichokes, and bring the water back to the boil. Cover, and boil over high heat for 20 minutes. Cool under cold running water.

centre leaves to expose the chokes and discard. Cut off the stems and, if they are tender, chop them coarsely and add them to the stuffing. Fill the centre of the artichokes with the stuffing and insert remaining stuffing between the leaves.

4 Place the stuffed artichokes upright in a saucepan and pour in the water, the remaining 2 tablespoons of olive oil, and 1/4 teaspoon each of the salt and pepper. Bring to a boil, and boil gently, covered, for 15 minutes. If the pan becomes dry and the artichokes begin to fry, add 2–3 tablespoons of water. Arrange the artichokes on a serving plate and serve with any remaining natural juices.

Asparagus in Mustard Sauce

ASPARAGUS is a good source of folic acid and Vitamin B. I peel the stalks for this recipe (so they are completely edible) and cook the asparagus in just enough water so that most of it has evaporated by the time the asparagus is cooked, thus preserving the vitamins and nutrients in the vegetable. The pungent mustard dressing should be served at room temperature.

SERVES 4

550 g (1 1/4 lb) asparagus (about 15 stalks)
3/4 cup water
1 tablespoon Dijon-style mustard
2 tablespoons vegetable oil
1/4 teaspoon freshly ground black pepper
1/2 teaspoon salt

1 Using a vegetable peeler, peel the asparagus stalks to remove the fibrous skin from the bottom third of the stalks. Cut the asparagus diagonally into 5–6 cm (2–3 in) pieces.

2 Place the asparagus in a stainless steel saucepan and add the water. Cover, bring to the boil, and boil for 3 minutes, until the asparagus is just tender and most of the liquid has evaporated.

3 Drain off any remaining water and place asparagus in a bowl. Add the mustard, oil, pepper and salt, and mix well. Serve at room temperature.

Beans and Escarole

THE cooked beans can be served warm with a little olive oil. Here, I have combined them with greens to enhance the flavour, lend colour, and make them more nutritious. In addition to the fibre in the beans, the escarole contains Vitamin A, present in all leafy green vegetables.

SERVES 4

225 g (8 oz) dried haricot beans

3/4 teaspoon salt

2 sprigs fresh thyme (or 1/2 teaspoon dried thyme leaves)

75 g (3 oz) ham, cut into 1 cm (1/2 in) dice

1 onion, peeled and cut into 2 cm (3/4 in) dice

2 tablespoons virgin olive oil

2 cloves garlic, peeled, crushed and finely chopped

1/4 teaspoon red pepper flakes

225 g (8 oz) escarole, washed and cut into 5 cm (2 in) pieces

1 Wash the beans and remove any pebbles or damaged beans.

2 In a pot, combine the beans with 4 cups cold water, salt, thyme, ham and onions. Bring to a boil for 10 minutes, cover, reduce the heat and simmer for about 1 1/2 hours, until the beans are tender and most of the water has been absorbed. There should be just enough water remaining so that the beans look moist and juicy.

3 Meanwhile, heat the oil in a frying pan, add the garlic and pepper flakes, and sauté for about 10 seconds. Then add the escarole (still wet from washing) and sauté for about 1 minute. Cover and cook over a medium heat for 5 to 6 minutes, until the greens soften, become tender, and render some of their juices.

4 At serving time, combine beans and escarole, rewarming them if necessary, and serve, if desired, with a little extra olive oil on each serving.

HOW TO COOK BEANS

It is a fallacy to believe that it takes a long time to cook dried beans. At the outset, there is no need to soak them beforehand, although you can do so for 1–2 hours if you like. I simply wash them, place them in a pot with cold water to cover, boil hard for 10–15 minutes, then cook them for 1–1 1/2 hours, depending on the type of beans.

Leeks with Tomato and Olive Oil

FRESH leeks, trimmed and cooked until just tender, are served with a tangy sauce flavoured with diced tomatoes, olive oil and Dijon-style mustard.

SERVES 4

4 medium to large leeks, about 550 g ($1^1/_4$ lb), trimmed and washed

1 ripe tomato, about 200 g (7 oz), peeled, seeded, and cut into 5 mm ($^1/_4$ in) pieces

3 tablespoons virgin olive oil

1 tablespoon red wine vinegar

1 tablespoon Dijon mustard

1 teaspoon Worcestershire sauce

$^1/_2$ teaspoon salt

$^1/_4$ teaspoon freshly ground black pepper

1 In a stainless steel saucepan, bring 2 cups of water to a boil. Add the leeks, bring back to the boil and boil gently, covered for 10 minutes or until tender.

2 Drain (reserving the juice for soup) and when cool enough to handle, squeeze the leeks to extract and reserve most of the remaining liquid.

3 Cut the leeks into 5 cm (2 in) pieces and arrange the pieces in a gratin dish, mixing them to combine the white and green parts.

4 Mix together the tomato, oil, vinegar, mustard, Worcestershire sauce, salt and pepper, and spoon the mixture over the leeks. Serve lukewarm or at room temperature.

A WORD ABOUT LEEKS

Cook leeks in unsalted water; the resulting leek stock has a wonderfully intense flavour, making it ideal to keep, refrigerated or frozen, for use in soups. Use most of the green from the leeks, trimming off and discarding only the tips of the leaves and wilted or damaged outer leaves. Leaving them attached at the root end, cut the leeks open and wash them thoroughly.

Steamed Chicory in Lemon Juice

BRAISED with lemon juice, chicory is a refreshing vegetable and it makes a wonderful first course. Served lukewarm with this seasoned juice, it is a great accompaniment to meat and fish.

SERVES 4

4 large or 8 small heads of chicory, about 350 g (12 oz)

1 tablespoon fresh lemon juice

3 2.5 cm (1 in) strips of lemon peel, removed with a vegetable peeler and cut into 12 pieces

1 tablespoon unsalted butter

1/4 cup water

1/2 teaspoon sugar

1/4 teaspoon salt

1 Rinse the chicory thoroughly and cut the heads in half lengthwise, if they are large, or leave them whole, if small.

2 Place the chicory (preferably in one layer) in a stainless steel saucepan. Add the lemon juice, lemon peel, butter, water, sugar, and salt.

3 Bring to a boil, and place an inverted plate slightly smaller than the pan over the chicory. Cover the pan with a lid, reduce the heat to low, and cook the chicory for 20 minutes, until just tender. Serve lukewarm.

A SPECIAL TECHNIQUE

In this recipe, I cook the chicory with a little lemon juice, lemon peel, butter, water, sugar, and salt. You will notice that there is only a little liquid in the bottom of the pan when you begin the cooking process. If a plate is placed on top of the chicory, however, to press down on them as cook, they will render a lot of juice, and, in fact, eventually finish cooking almost immersed in their own cooking liquid.

Sautéed Aubergine Rolls

THIS is a great party dish, perfect on a buffet table. The aubergine can be sautéed and stuffed ahead and the filling mixture changed at will to accommodate leftover meat or fish. The vinaigrette tomatoes, delicious with the aubergine, are also good with poached fish or mixed with a green salad.

SERVES 4

1/4 cup corn oil

1 aubergine, 45 g (1 lb), cut into 16 slices, each about 1 cm (3/8 in) thick

Salt and freshly ground black pepper to taste

3 tablespoons olive oil

1 small onion, about 75 g (3 oz), chopped

75 g (3 oz) mushrooms, chopped

2–3 large cloves garlic, peeled, crushed and finely chopped

100 g (4 oz) Monterey Jack or Cheddar cheese, coarsely chopped or grated

3 tablespoons golden raisins

1 tablespoon Worcestershire sauce

1/2 teaspoon salt

1/2 teaspoon freshly ground black pepper

4 tablespoons chopped chives

Vinaigrette Tomatoes

2 large ripe tomatoes, about 45 g (1 lb)

1 small onion, about 75 g (3 oz), chopped

2 teaspoons red wine vinegar

2 tablespoons virgin olive oil

1/2 teaspoon salt

1/4 teaspoon freshly ground black pepper

1 Heat 2 tablespoons of the corn oil in a non-stick frying pan and add 8 slices of the aubergine. Sprinkle lightly with salt and pepper, and cook for 5 minutes on each side over a medium heat. Remove to a dish and repeat with the remaining aubergine. Set aside.

2 Heat 2 tablespoons of the olive oil in a frying pan and sauté the onion in the hot oil for 1 minute. Add the mushrooms and sauté for another minute. Stir in the garlic and remove from the heat.

3 In a bowl, combine the cheese with the onion-mushroom mixture and mix in the raisins, Worcestershire sauce, salt, pepper, 3 tablespoons of chives, and the remaining tablespoon of olive oil. Divide the mixture between the 16 slices of aubergine and roll to form stuffed aubergine rolls.

For vinaigrette tomatoes:

1 Cut the tomatoes in half horizontally and gently squeeze out the seeds. Chop into 5 mm (1/4 in) pieces.

2 In a bowl, combine the chopped tomatoes, onions, vinegar, oil, salt, and pepper.

3 To serve, spread the tomato mixture on a large serving plate and arrange the aubergine rolls on top. Sprinkle with the remaining tablespoon of chives and serve at room temperature with some of the tomato mixture.

Gratin of Spring Onions

THESE spring onions can be prepared ahead, ready for reheating at the last minute. If you do, increase the baking time by 5 minutes to ensure they are hot.

SERVES 4

4 bunches of spring onions, 550 g (1 1/4 lb), about 6 spring onions to the bunch
1 cup water
1/2 cup full-fat milk
1/2 slice fresh bread
2 tablespoons grated Parmesan cheese
1/4 teaspoon salt
1/4 teaspoon freshly ground black pepper

1 Pre-heat the oven to gas mark 8, 450°F (230°C).

2 Remove and discard the top 5 cm (2 in) and any damaged or wilted leaves from the spring onions. Rinse them thoroughly.

3 Place the spring onions in a stainless steel saucepan with the water. Bring to a boil, cover and cook over a high heat for 5 minutes. Most of the liquid will have evaporated.

4 Arrange the spring onions in a shallow dish and pour the milk over them. Break the bread into pieces, place in the bowl of a food processor, and process them momentarily, just until crumbed. (You should have 1/4 cup.)

Pasta with Courgettes

I MAKE this extra simple pasta sauce with courgettes, garlic, salt, pepper and olive oil. The combination of vegetables and cooking liquid creates a rich, satisfying, colourful pasta sauce that is not too calorific.

SERVES 4

175 g (6 oz) farfalle (bow-tie shaped) pasta

2 small courgettes, about 250 g (9 oz)

3 tablespoons virgin olive oil

8 cloves garlic, peeled and sliced

1/2 teaspoon salt

1/4 teaspoon freshly ground black pepper

2 tablespoons grated Parmesan cheese

1 Bring 10 cups of water to a boil in a large saucepan. Add the farfalle and cook over high heat for 13 to 15 minutes, until done as desired.

2 Meanwhile, wash the courgettes and cut them in half lengthwise and then into 5 mm (1/4 in) slices. Then stack up the slices and cut them into 5 mm (1/4 in) sticks. You should have 2 cups.

3 Heat the olive oil in a frying pan. When hot, sauté the courgette sticks over a high heat for 4 minutes, until lightly browned and cooked through. Add the garlic and sauté for 30 seconds longer.

4 When the pasta is cooked, remove 1/3 cup of the cooking liquid and place it in a bowl large enough to hold the pasta. Drain the pasta through a colander and add it to the bowl. Add the courgettes, salt, and pepper, and toss to combine. Serve with the grated cheese.

5 In a small bowl, mix together the breadcrumbs, cheese, salt, and pepper, and sprinkle the mixture over the spring onions. Bake in the pre-heated oven for 10 minutes.

Pasta with Fresh Vegetable Sauce

HERE'S a low-calorie pasta dish that can be made in about 20 minutes. Remember to put the pasta cooking water on to boil before you begin this recipe as it only takes about 7 minutes to make the sauce and about the same amount of time to cook the pasta.

SERVES 4

225 g (8 oz) spaghetti

1/4 cup virgin olive oil

1 large red onion, peeled and thinly sliced (1 1/2 cups)

1 small aubergine, about 175 g (6 oz), cut into 1 cm (1/2 in) pieces

3-4 cloves garlic, peeled, crushed and finely chopped

2 ripe beef tomatoes, about 350 g (12 oz), seeded and cut into 1 cm (1/2 in) pieces

1 teaspoon salt

1/2 teaspoon freshly ground black pepper

2 tablespoons coarsely chopped parsley

About 2 tablespoons grated Parmesan cheese

1 Bring 3.4 litres (6 pints) of water to the boil. Add the pasta, return the water to the boil and cook for about 8 minutes, until the pasta is just tender.

2 Meanwhile, heat the olive oil in a large saucepan and sauté the onions and aubergine until soft and lightly browned, 6 to 7 minutes. Remove the pan from the heat and mix in the garlic. Add the tomatoes, salt, and pepper; mix thoroughly and set aside.

3 Remove 1/3 cup of pasta cooking liquid and add it to the aubergine mixture. Drain the pasta, add it to the saucepan and toss to coat it with the vegetables.

4 Divide between four plates, sprinkle with the parsley, and serve with cheese.

PREVENTING STICKY PASTA

Notice that I don't salt the pasta cooking water. I see no difference in the cooking process, and I'd rather save the salt for use in the sauce. To prevent the cooked pasta from sticking together or being too dense, I reserve a little of the pasta cooking water and add it to the vegetables before tossing them with the pasta.

Mushroom-stuffed Potato Pancakes

POTATO pancakes – conventionally deep-fried – often contain as many as 500 calories each. Sautéed simply in a little oil in a non-stick frying pan, as they are here, they amount to about 200 calories for each portion. I serve them as a first course but they make a delightful main course, too.

SERVES 6

4–5 potatoes, about 750 g (1½ lb), cleaned

¾ teaspoon salt

½ teaspoon freshly ground black pepper

5 tablespoons vegetable oil

4 shallots, peeled and sliced

2 cloves garlic, peeled, crushed and finely chopped

100 g (4 oz) mushrooms, chopped

12 oil-cured black olives, pitted and cut into 1 cm (½ in) dice

1 Place the potatoes in a saucepan and cover with cool water. Bring to the boil, and cook gently for 30 minutes or until tender. Remove and let the potatoes cool. Then peel and push through a food mill or blend to a purée in a food processor. Season with ½ teaspoon of salt and ¼ teaspoon of pepper.

2 Meanwhile, in a large frying pan or saucepan heat 1 tablespoon of oil, add shallots and sauté for one minute. Add garlic and mushrooms, and cook for about 3 minutes, until the moisture is almost gone. Remove from the heat and add the olives and remaining salt and pepper. Cool.

3 Divide the cold potato purée into 24 equal-sized balls. Arrange the balls about 15 cm (6 in) apart on a large sheet of plastic wrap. Cover with a second piece of plastic and press on each ball to create a pancake about 6 cm (3 in) in diameter and 5 mm (¼ in) thick. Spoon 1 tablespoon of the mixture on 12 pancakes; cover with the remaining pancakes.

4 Heat the remaining 4 tablespoons of oil in two large non-stick frying pans over medium to high heat. When hot, add the filled pancakes in a single layer and cook them for about 3 minutes. Turn carefully with a large spatula and cook for about 3 minutes on the other side. Remove to a serving platter and serve immediately or set aside and reheat in the oven or under the grill, just before serving.

Potato Crêpes with Caviar

THESE crêpes are served covered with caviar, the amount adjusted to suit your purse. I've used moderately expensive red caviar. Then, to make the dish superlative, a little of the expensive black caviar from sturgeon is placed in the centre of each crêpe for that extra special occasion.

SERVES 4

Crêpes
1 large potato, about 250 g (9 oz)
2 large whole eggs plus 1 egg white
1/3 cup milk
1/4 teaspoon salt
1/8 teaspoon Tabasco sauce
2 tablespoons flour
4 tablespoons corn oil

Garnishes
About 225 g (8 oz) natural red salmon caviar
1 cup sour cream
1 tablespoon finely chopped chives
About 50 g (2 oz) Beluga, Osetra, or Sevruga caviar (Look for 'Malossol', which means lightly salted)

For crêpes:

1 Place the potato in a saucepan with water to cover and bring to a boil Cover, reduce the heat, and boil gently for 30 minutes, until the potato is tender. Drain, peel, and press through a food mill into a bowl.

2 Add the whole eggs and egg white and mix well with a whisk. Then mix in the milk, salt and Tabasco sauce.

3 In a frying pan, heat 2 teaspoons of oil. When hot, add about 1/4 cup of the crépe mixture, which should spread to create a circle about 10–13 cm (4 1/2–5 in) in diameter. Cook over a medium heat for about 2 minutes on each side.

4 Transfer to a baking sheet and set aside in a warm oven while you make five more crêpes with the remaining batter and oil.

For garnishes:

1 To serve, spread the entire top surface of the lukewarm crêpes with red caviar, extending it to the edge of each crepe. Mound 2 tablespoons of sour cream in the centre of each crêpe, and sprinkle it with chives. Finally, place about 1 1/2 teaspoons of black caviar in the centre of the sour cream mound. Serve immediately.

Crab Cakes with Avocado Sauce

ALTHOUGH I use real crabmeat for my crabmeat cakes, you can substitute *surimi,* the product of an old Japanese procedure that involves making crabmeat with protein and less exotic fish like pollack and cod. This imitation crabmeat is widely available in markets and would be good prepared like this. Be sure to add the breadcrumbs at the end of the mixing process and to toss them very lightly.

SERVES 4

Crab Cakes

225 g (8 oz) crabmeat

1/4 teaspoon freshly ground black pepper

1/4 teaspoon dried thyme

1 tablespoon chives

1/8 teaspoon Tabasco sauce

1/4 teaspoon salt

3 tablespoons mayonnaise

1 1/2 slices bread, processed to make 3/4 cup crumbs

2 tablespoons groundnut oil

Avocado Sauce

1 ripe tomato, about 150 g (5 oz)

1 small ripe avocado, about 175 g (6 oz)

1 tablespoon red wine vinegar

2 tablespoons groundnut oil

1/4 teaspoon freshly ground black pepper

1/4 teaspoon salt

3 tablespoons water

1 tablespoon chopped chives, for garnish

For crab cakes:

1 Cut the crabmeat into 5 mm (1/4 in) pieces. (You should have 1 1/2 lightly packed cups.)

2 In a bowl, mix the crabmeat with the pepper, thyme, chives, Tabasco, salt and mayonnaise. Add the breadcrumbs and toss them likely into the mixture. Divide the mixture and form it into four patties, each about 2.5 cm (1 in) thick and weighing about 15 g (1/2 oz). Handle the mxiture gently; it should barely hold together .

3 In a large frying pan, heat the oil. When hot, place the patties carefully in the pan and sauté them gently in the oil over a medium heat for 3 to 4 minutes on each side.

For avocado sauce:

1 While the crabmeat cakes are cooking, skin, seed, and coarsely chop the tomato. Peel and pit the avocado and coarsely chop it. Place the chopped toma-

toes and avocado in a bowl and add the vinegar, groundnut oil, pepper, salt and water.

2 To serve, spoon some sauce onto four individual plates, sprinkle with chives and place a patty on top. Serve immediately.

Clam Croquettes

I SERVE these clam croquettes on salad greens, which absorb some of their richness and help balance the dish. You can substitute cockles, pieces of oyster or raw shrimp for the clams in this recipe. There are just enough breadcrumbs and mayonnaise to bind the mixture together so that it can be formed into patties and sautéed. Use a low-calorie mayonnaise to eliminate a few additional calories.

SERVES 4

1 tablespoon virgin olive oil

1 small onion, about 50 g (2 oz), peeled and chopped

2 spring onions, minced

225 g (8 oz) shelled fresh clams, drained and cut into 5 mm (1/4 in) pieces

1/2 teaspoon chopped Jalapeño or chilli pepper

2 tablespoons mayonnaise

1/4 teaspoon Tabasco sauce

1/4 teaspoon salt

3 slices white bread

3 tablespoons safflower oil

Seasoned Salad

1 1/2 cups mixture of salad greens, washed and thoroughly dried

1 tablespoon groundnut oil

1 teaspoon red wine vinegar

1/8 teaspoon salt

1/8 teaspoon freshly ground black pepper

For croquettes:

1 Heat the olive oil in a frying pan. When hot, add the onions and spring onions, and sauté for 1 minute.

2 Remove from the heat and place in a bowl. Stir in the clams, Jalapeño pepper, mayonnaise, Tabasco and salt, and mix well.

3 Break the bread slices into pieces and place them in the bowl of a food processor. Process briefly, until just crumbed. You should have about 1 1/2 cups of fresh breadcrumbs. Add the crumbs to the mixture in the bowl and toss them lightly. Form the mixture into twelve patties.

4 Heat half the safflower oil in a frying pan. When hot, add six patties and sauté for $2^1/_2$ minutes on each side. Repeat with the remainder of the oil and patties.

For seasoned salad:
1 In a bowl, toss the salad greens with the oil, vinegar, salt, and pepper.

2 Arrange the greens on four individual plates and top each serving with 3 croquettes. Serve.

Smoked Salmon Mould

THIS is an ideal party dish because it can and should be made ahead. After lining the moulds with plastic wrap, the layers of filling are added. The compacted mixture can be removed immediately from the moulds and stored until serving time in the plastic wrap.

SERVES 4

4 teaspoons chopped chives
6 tablespoons cream cheese
4 large radishes, cut into thin slices
150 g (5 oz) smoked salmon
$^1/_8$ teaspoon freshly ground black pepper
4 slices bread, toasted and cut into triangles

1 Line four $^1/_2$-cup moulds with plastic wrap. Place 1 teaspoon of chives and 2 teaspoons of cream cheese in the bottom of each mould, pressing on the cheese to imbed the chives.

2 Arrange about 3 slices of radish on top of the cheese in each cup and press down again to make the mixture more compact. Place about $^1/_8$ of the fish ($1^1/_2$ tablespoons) on top of each and add another 2 teaspoons of cream cheese. Sprinkle with the pepper, and add another layer of fish and a layer of radish.

VARIATIONS

In this recipe, I use smoked salmon although another type of smoked fish can be substituted. In place of the radishes, you can layer cucumbers or other vegetables in the moulds; caviar, arranged between layers of cream cheese, is even a possibility here. If you're counting calories, the cream cheese can be replaced with cottage cheese.

3 Cover with plastic wrap and press on the mixture to make it more compact. Refrigerate until serving time.

4 To serve, unmould, remove the plastic wrap and serve with toast triangle

Steamed Cod on Tapenade

TAPENADE comes from the word *tapeno,* which means 'capers' in Provence, where this concoction originated. I add coarsely chopped figs to my version, which gives it an interesting taste of sweetness. The steamed cod (or another variety of fish, if you prefer) is placed directly on the strongly flavoured tapenade.

SERVES 4

Tapenade

2/3 cup black oil-cured olives, pitted and finely chopped

8 anchovy fillets in oil, drained, and finely chopped

2 tablespoons capers, drained, rinsed under cool tap water and finely chopped

2 small black dried figs, finely chopped

4 tablespoons virgin olive oil

1/4 teaspoon freshly ground black pepper

2 tablespoons water

4 thick cod fillets, 150 g (5 oz) each

6 basil leaves, for garnish

A piece of tomato skin, cut into strips, for garnish

For tapenade:

1 In a bowl mix together the olives, anchovies, capers, figs, olive oil, and pepper. Set aside.

For cod:

1 Place about 2.5 cm (1 in) of water in a steamer and bring it to a strong boil.

STEAMING TECHNIQUE

I steam the fish in a conventional steamer, but, if you don't have one, place it in a stainless steel pan containing approximately 1 cm (1/2 in) of water and cook it, covered, for about 2 minutes on each side. By the time the fish has finished cooking most of the water will have evaporated and the fish will, in a sense, be steamed.

Arrange the fish in a single layer on a plate, and place the plate in the steamer. Steam the fish, covered, for 4 to 5 minutes.

2 Meanwhile, arrange the tapenade mixture on individual plates. When the fish pieces are cooked, place one in the centre of each plate.

3 Thinly slice the basil leaves to make a chiffonade and sprinkle over the cod. Arrange the tomato strips on top and serve.

Sautéed Salmon on Greens

SALMON is a great seafood choice because it is available practically year round from your fishmonger. High in *omega 3*, salmon is recommended by doctors and is especially versatile, accommodating itself to poaching, braising, sauteeing, and grilling.

SERVES 4

4 skinless, boneless salmon fillet steaks, about 150 g (5 oz) each

4 tablespoons virgin oil

225 g (8 oz) spinach, thoroughly cleaned

3/4 teaspoon salt

1/4 teaspoon freshly ground black pepper

1/2 cup chopped onion

3 ripe tomatoes, about 550 g (1 1/4 lb), peeled, seeded and cut into 1 cm (1/2 in) pieces

1 tablespoon coarsely chopped flat-leaf parsley

SPECIAL TECHNIQUES

Notice that the steaks are marinated in a little olive oil; that light coating of fat is all that is required to cook them, which only takes a couple of minutes in a very hot frying pan. The spinach is cooked dry, the only moisture being the small amount of water clinging to the leaves after the vegetable is washed; this helps retain nutrients, colour, and vitamins. And the tomatoes are also lightly sauteed so they keep their fresh, sweet taste.

1 Arrange the salmon steaks on a plate, spoon 1 tablespoon olive oil over them, cover with plastic wrap and refrigerate.

2 In a frying pan, heat 1 tablespoon of the remaining olive oil. When hot, sauté the spinach for $1^1/_2$ minutes. Mix in $^1/_4$ teaspoon of the salt and $^1/_8$ teaspoon of the pepper, and divide the spinach among four plates.

3 Heat the remaining 2 tablespoons of olive oil in the frying pan and sauté the onion for 1 minute. Add the tomatoes, $^1/_4$ teaspoon of the salt, and $^1/_8$ teaspoon of the pepper, and cook for about 30 seconds. Set aside.

4 Remove the salmon from the refrigerator, and sprinkle it with the remaining $^1/_4$ teaspoon salt. Heat a non-stick frying pan until very hot, add the salmon steaks, and sauté for $1^1/_2$ minutes on each side. Let rest in the pan for a few minutes before serving.

5 Spoon some of the onion-tomato mixture over the spinach and top with salmon. Sprinkle with parsley and serve immediately.

Tuna Tartare on Marinated Cucumbers

THE tartare is served on a fresh-tasting garnish composed of sliced cucumber, vinegar, minced chives, peanut oil, and salt. Delicious and attractive, this simple but sophisticated dish makes a great first course. The tuna should be chopped by hand rather than in a food processor.

SERVES 4

450 g (1 lb) completely cleaned raw tuna
1 large shallot, peeled and finely chopped
2 cloves garlic, peeled, crushed and finely chopped
1 teaspoon salt
$^1/_2$ teaspoon freshly ground black pepper
2 tablespoons virgin olive oil
$1^1/_2$ teaspoons white vinegar
$^1/_4$ teaspoons Tabasco sauce

Cucumber Garnish
1 cucumber, about 350 g (12 oz)
1 teaspoon vinegar
1 teaspoon peanut oil
$^1/_4$ teaspoon salt
3 tablespoons minced chives, for garnish

1 Reserve four small slices, 25 g (1 oz) each of the tuna and chop the remainder by hand into 5 mm (1/4 in) dice. Place one of the reserved slices of tuna between two sheets of plastic wrap, and pound it into a thin round about 10 cm (4 in) in diameter. Repeat with the other three slices.

2 Remove the top sheet of plastic wrap from the slices, and season them lightly with salt. Set aside.

3 In a bowl mix the chopped tuna with the shallots, garlic, salt, pepper, olive oil, vinegar, and Tabasco. (Mixed with vinegar, the chopped tuna will 'whiten' somewhat, becoming opaque. This is because the acidic acid in the vinegar coagulates, thus 'cooking' the protein in the tuna.)

For cucumber garnish:
1 Peel the cucumber and cut long, thin strips from it with a vegetable peeler on all sides until you come to the seeds. Discard the seeds, and mix the strips with the vinegar, oil, and salt.

2 To serve, divide the garnish among four plates. Form the chopped tuna mixture into 4 balls and place one on top of the cucumber on each of the plates. Wrap a slice of tuna around each tuna ball, sprinkle with the chives, and serve.

TUNA TARTARE

Tuna tartare is a modern recipe inspired by Japanese *sashimi*. Use only super-fresh fish purchased from a reputable fishmonger, and if you are afraid of any type of parasites, request that your fishmonger freeze the fish you buy for a minimum of 5 to 7 days at 0 degrees or less, a bit colder than most home freezers can be set.

Trout Sauté Terry

FRESH farm-raised trout are best for this recipe. I created a sauce adding mushrooms, tomatoes, olive pieces and diced lemon to the pan drippings. The result is not only delicious, but beautiful to look at.

SERVES 4

2 tablespoons unsalted butter

2 tablespoons corn oil

4 fresh trout, about 350 g (12 oz) each, cleaned and gutted

1/2 teaspoon salt

1/2 teaspoon freshly ground black pepper

1 1/2 cups diced mushrooms (3 or 4 large mushrooms)

1 large tomato, 225 g (8 oz), halved, seeded and cut into 1 cm (1/2 in) pieces

24 oil-cured olives, pitted and cut into 5 mm (3/8 in) dice

1 small lemon, peeled and cut into 5 mm (3/8 in) dice (1/4 cup)

2 tablespoons chopped chives

1 Heat the butter and oil in one very large or two 23 cm (9 in) non-stick frying pans. Pat the trout dry and place them in the hot butter. Sprinkle with the salt and pepper and cook over a medium to high heat, covered, for 4 minutes. Then turn and cook on the other side for 4 minutes.

2 Transfer the trout to a platter, and set it aside in a warm place. The trout can be served with the bone in and head left on, or it can be boned and returned to the serving platter before being served.

3 To the drippings in the pan, add the mushrooms. Sauté for 1 minute, then add the diced tomatoes and sauté for 1 minute longer. Add the olive pieces and the diced lemon, and toss well. Spoon the contents of the pan over the trout and serve.

Sautéed Scallops with Mangetouts

THIS red, green and white-coloured dish is perfect for the holidays, and can be served as a first course. Ready in a few minutes, the mangetouts are cooked in a minimum of water and the scallops require only brief sautéeing at the last moment.

SERVES 4

226g (8 oz) mangetouts, trimmed
1/4 cup water
1/2 red pepper, 100 g (4 oz)
1 tablespoon unsalted butter
2 tablespoons virgin olive oil
350 g (12 oz) small scallops
1/4 teaspoon salt
1/4 teaspoon freshly ground black pepper
1/2 teaspoon Tabasco sauce

1 Place the mangetouts in one very large or two smaller frying pans with the water. Cook, covered, for 2 minutes, and then uncover and cook until dry.

2 Meanwhile, remove the skin from the pepper with a vegetable peeler and cut the flesh into 5 mm (1/4 in) dice. Add the red pepper to the mangetouts and half the butter and oil. Sauté over a high heat for 2 minutes. Arrange on individual plates.

3 Sprinkle the scallops with the salt and pepper, and heat the remaining butter and oil in a frying pan. When very hot, add the scallops and the Tabasco sauce, and sauté over very high heat for 2–3 minutes.

4 Arrange the scallops on the mangetouts and serve immediately.

NUTRITIONAL INFORMATION
The mangetouts are cooked very quickly – just until the water evaporates – so that all the nutrients are left behind. The mangetouts are low in calories and high in fibre and Vitamin A, and the red pepper, also low in calories, is high in Vitamin C.

Hot Prawns on Spinach

THE prawns are shelled in this recipe, but I often make this dish as home with unshelled prawns, which the family peels right at the table. For guests, it is better to buy the prawns shelled or to shell them yourself. They only take a few minutes to cook this way and are easier to eat. Remember to cook the greens first.

SERVES 4

450 g (1 lb) large prawns (about 16), unshelled
1/2 teaspoon dried thyme
1/2 teaspoon dried oregano
1 teaspoon dried tarragon
1/4 teaspoon dried ground coriander
1/4 teaspoon freshly ground black pepper
1/8 teaspoon cayenne pepper
2 tablespoons virgin olive oil

Greens
2 tablespoons virgin olive oil
275 g (10 oz) cleaned spinach
1/4 teaspoon salt
1/4 teaspoon freshly ground black pepper

1 Shell the prawns and sprinkle them with the thyme, oregano, tarragon, coriander, and peppers. Place them in a single layer in a dish and sprinkle with the oil. Set aside.

For greens:
1 In a saucepan, heat 2 tablespoons olive oil. When hot, sauté the spinach for 2 minutes. Add the salt and pepper and combine. Divide among four plates

2 Heat an aluminium or cast iron frying pan until very, very hot. Place the oiled prawns in one layer in the pan, and cook over a high heat for 1 minute. Turn and cook for 1 1/2 minutes on the other side.

3 To serve, place 4 prawns on top of the greens on each plate. Add 2 tablespoons of water to the juices in the pan and mix to deglaze. Pour the juices over the prawns and serve.

Mussels Gratinée

THESE mussels are excellent as a first course. They can be opened up to a day ahead, the seasonings arranged on top, and then the dish refrigerated until ready to place under the grill. The juices released by the mussels can be frozen for use in soups or sauces.

SERVES 4

24 mussels, about 1 kg (2 lb)
3 cloves garlic, peeled
1/2 cup loose flat-leaf parsley
2 slices white bread
1/8 teaspoon salt
1/4 teaspoon freshly ground black pepper
2 tablespoons virgin olive oil
A few drops of Tabasco sauce (optional)

1 To open the mussels, place them in a pot without any liquid or seasonings and cook over high heat, covered, for 6-8 minutes, just until they have opened and released their juices. (Do not over-cook because they will be re-cooked under the grill at serving time.) Discard any mussels that fail to open.

2 Remove and discard the empty shell of each cooked mussel and arrange the mussels in the half shells on a baking sheet.

3 Place garlic and parsley in the bowl of a food processor and process until coarsely chopped. Add the 2 slices of bread and process until the mixture is finely chopped and fluffy.

4 Transfer the parsley-bread mixture to a mixing bowl and add the salt, pepper, olive oil, and, if desired, Tabasco. Mix the ingredients lightly with your fingers or a fork, tossing them gently so they are moistened with the oil but still fluffy. Sprinkle the mixture over the mussels.

5 At serving time, place the mussels under the grill for 2 to 3 minutes, until nicely browned on top and warm inside.

Beef Carpaccio

IN my version of *Carpaccio*, I eliminate the traditional mayonnaise accompaniment and serve the beef with a little olive oil, black pepper, red onion, basil leaves, and Parmesan cheese. Quick and easy to prepare, it is delicious and attractive.

SERVES 4

1 350 g (12 oz) piece beef sirloin, sinew and fat removed

1/2 teaspoon salt

1/2 teaspoon freshly ground black pepper

1 small red onion or piece of red onion, about 50 g (2 oz), very thinly sliced

10 large basil leaves, shredded into thin strips

40 g (1 1/2 oz) Parmesan cheese (in a chunk)

4 tablespoons extra virgin olive oil

1 Clean any remaining fat from the exterior of the meat – you should have 225–250 g (8 to 9 oz) and cut it into four pieces, each about 50 g (2 oz).

2 Butterfly each piece and pound it between two pieces of plastic wrap until it is quite thin and about 18–20 cm (7 to 8 in) in diameter. Arrange a piece on each of four plates and sprinkle it with the salt and pepper.

3 Place the onion slices in a colander and rinse under cold water. Pat dry and distribute over the meat; sprinkle the shredded basil on top.

4 Using a vegetable peeler, cut shavings of the cheese and let them drop directly on top of the meat. Sprinkle 1 tablespoon of oil on each portion and serve immediately.

A WORD ABOUT CARPACCIO

Vittore Carpaccio was a fifteenth century Venetian painter who favoured red and white on his canvasses. When the creators of this dish featuring thinly pounded raw beef – bright red, of course – decided to serve it with a strip of mayonnaise, it seemed appropriate to name it after the painter most associated with these two colours.

Main Course

Moules Maison
Red Snapper in Potato Jackets
Salmon Pojarski
Couscous of Lobster
Trout on Ratatouille
Chicken and Seafood Paella
Chicken Legs with Wine and Yams
Chicken in Tarragon Sauce
Grilled Chicken with Cabbage Anchoïade
Poule au Pot
Poulet au Vin Rouge
Brown Rice Chicken Fricassee
Grilled Quail on Quinoa with Sunflower Seeds
Roasted Turkey with Mushroom Stuffing
Ragout of Rabbit
Veal Chops with Mushrooms
Veal Roast with Artichokes
Wine Merchant Steak
Spicy Beef Shell Roast
Grilled Lamb Chops with Savory
Irish Lamb Stew
Grilled Leg of Lamb
Saucisses au Chou on Lentils
Braised Pork Cocotte
Smoked Pork Roast with Mustard-Honey Glaze

Moules Maison

THIS is the simplest way to cook mussels - all the ingredients are combined in a saucepan and the mixture is cooked together for a few minutes. There is enough juice in the mussels, mushrooms and tomatoes to create a nice sauce. Serve this dish for casual dining or as a first course.

SERVES 4

1.75 kg (4 lb) mussels, cleaned

6 plum tomatoes, 450 g (1 lb), seeded and cut into 4 cm (1 1/2 in) cubes

6 spring onions, trimmed and cut into 5 mm (1/4 in) dice

225 g (8 oz) mushrooms, cut into 1 cm (1/2 in) dice

2 onions, 225 g (8 oz), peeled and coarsely chopped

8 cloves garlic, peeled and sliced

1 cup dry white wine

4 tablespoons virgin olive oil

1 1/2 teaspoons Tabasco sauce

1/2 teaspoon salt or to taste

1/4 cup coarsely chopped flat-leaf parsley

1 Place the mussels, tomatoes, spring onions, mushrooms, onions, garlic, wine, olive oil, Tabasco and salt in a large saucepan and bring to the boil. Cover and cook 6-7 minutes, stirring occasionally, until all the mussels have opened. (Remove and discard any that fail to open.)

2 Divide the mussels among four dishes and either serve as is, or remove and discard the shell halves without meat and serve the mussels in the half shell. Spoon sauce over the mussels, sprinkle them with parsley, and serve with French fries.

Red Snapper in Potato Jackets

COOKED between layers of sliced potato, these moist fish fillets make an impressive main course. The courgette garnish makes a good first course, too. Serve just as they emerge from the frying pan, while the potatoes are still crisp.

SERVES 4

2 large potatoes, about 450 g (1 lb)

4 2.5 cm (1 in) thick fish fillets, 150 g (5 oz) each, from red snapper, black fish, or sea bass

1/4 teaspoon salt

1/8 teaspoon freshly ground black pepper

Courgette Garnish

1 medium courgette, about 225 g (8 oz)

3 tablespoons groundnut oil

1 tablespoon soy sauce

2 tablespoons virgin olive oil

2 tablespoons chopped parlsey

VARIATIONS

Any variety of thick fish fillet will work here. If you can't get a sea-water fish like snapper, use trout instead, altering the cooking time to accommodate variations in thickness. Obviously, the most important consideration when selecting the fish is freshnesss.

USING A MANDOLINE

* I use a mandoline, a professional slicer made of stainless steel, but any slicer (including the 1 mm blade on a food processor) will work well.

1 Peel the potatoes and thinly slice them lengthwise.* (You should have about 50 slices.) Wash potatoes, drain off water, and pat slices dry with paper towels.

2 Place 4 pieces of plastic wrap (each 15 cm (6 in square) on the table. Arrange 6 overlapping slices of potato in the centre of each square and place a piece of fish on top. Sprinkle with the salt and pepper. Arrange another 6 slices of potato, also overlapping, on top of the fish and fold the plastic around them so they are completely wrapped. Refrigerate until ready to cook (not too far ahead, or the potatoes will discolour), or cook immediately.

3 Pre-heat the oven to gas mark 6, 400°F (200°C). Cut the courgette into 5 cm (2 in) chunks, then into 3 mm (1/8 in) slices, and, finally, into a julienne. Spread the courgette out on a tray and place in the pre-heated oven for 5–6 minutes to soften it. Transfer the courgette to a bowl and toss it with 1 tablespoon of peanut oil and the soy sauce.

4. At cooking time, divide 2 tablespoons each of olive oil and groundnut oil between 2 non-stick frying pans and place over medium heat. Carefully unwrap the potato-fish packages and, with a large spatula, transfer them to the frying pans, placing two in each pan. Sauté 5 minutes, then carefully turn (so the arrangement is not disturbed), and sauté for 5 minutes or until potatoes are nicely browned.

5 To serve, arrange the courgette in a circle to border the plate and place the fish in potato jackets in the centre. Sprinkle with parsley and serve.

Salmon Pojarski

POJARSKI of salmon used to be made with a purée of salmon, egg yolks, bread and cream. In my updated recipe, the salmon is coarsely chopped, yielding a better texture, and is held together with a little bread and an egg white. Instead of moistening the bread with cream (doing a *panade*), I use chicken stock and other seasonings, and add raw mushrooms, which give moisture and taste to the patties. Don't add the mushrooms more than a few hours ahead, however, as they tend to bleed and discolour the mixture. The salmon is served with a refreshing crudité sauce that is also good with grilled poultry or meat

SERVES 4

Crudité Sauce

1/2 cucumber, peeled, seeded and finely chopped

1/3 red pepper

2 spring onions

1 clove garlic, peeled, crushed and finely chopped

2 tablespoons vinegar

1/3 cup vinegar

1 teaspoon sugar

1/2 teaspoon salt

1/8 teaspoon freshly ground black pepper

1/8 teaspoon Tabasco sauce

Patties

1 medium onion, 100 g (4 oz)

50 g (2 oz) mushrooms

1 tablespoon corn oil

3 tablespoons water

2 slices white bread, 50 g (2 oz)

1/3 cup chicken stock, preferably home-made (see Chicken Broth, page 31)

450 g (1 lb) salmon, cleaned of skin, sinew and bones (400 g/14 oz trimmed)

1 egg white

2 tablespoons coarsely chopped parsley

2 tablespoons chopped chives

1/2 teaspoon salt

1/4 teaspoon freshly ground black pepper

For sauce:

1 Peel the cucumber, remove the seeds and chop finely. Place in a large bowl.

2 Using a vegetable peeler, remove the skin from the pepper and finely chop the flesh. Add to the cucumber.

3 Mince the spring onions finely and add to the bowl along with the garlic, vinegar, water, sugar salt, pepper and Tabasco. Sed aside until ready to serve.

For salmon patties:

1 Coarsely chop the onions and mushrooms. You should have 1 cup of each. Combine the onions, oil and water in a frying pan, and bring to the boil. Cook, covered, for 1 minute. Uncover, and add the mushrooms. Cook until most of the moisture has evaporated and the onions and mushrooms are beginning to fry. Cool.

2 Place the bread in a food processor, and process to make 1 cup breadcrumbs. Transfer to a bowl, and mix in the stock.

3 Coarsely chop the salmon, cutting it into 5 mm (1/4 in) pieces. Add the salmon along with the cooked onions and mushrooms, egg white, parsley, chives, salt and pepper. Mix until well combined. Divide the mixture into four equal parts, each about 175 g (6 oz) and form into round or oval patties. (The mixture will be soft, so dampen your hands to help in the moulding process.) Arrange the patties on an ovenproof plate the fits into a steamer (mine is bamboo).

4 Steam, covered, over boiling water for 6–7 minutes. They should still be moist in the centre after steaming. Serve with the sauce.

SALMON

Salmon is one of the fatty fish recommended by doctors; it tends to lower fat in the blood and reduce triglycerides. Potatoes, a complex carbohydrate high in potassium, contain only 20 calories per 26 g (1 oz), while broccoli is loaded with Vitamins C and A, potassium and iron.

Couscous of Lobster

THIS impressive dish for a very special occasion combines lobster meat with a tasty couscous and is served with fresh chive sauce. For a decorative presentation, the shells from the bodies of the lobsters can be used as dishes.

SERVES 4

2 lobsters 1 kg (2 lb) each, preferably female

2 tablespoons virgin olive oil

1 medium onion, peeled and chopped (1 cup)

1/2 cup tomalley (liver) and coral (eggs), if lobster is a female

1 1/2 cups, about 275 g (10 oz) couscous

1/2 teaspoon salt

1/4 teaspoon freshly ground black pepper

Chive Sauce

1/2 cup reduced lobster stock

1/4 cup virgin olive oil

4 tablespoons finely chopped chives

1/8 teaspoon salt

1/8 teaspoon freshly ground black pepper

COOKING LOBSTER

The lobster is cooked initially for only 8 minutes – just enough so that it can be removed from the shell. Then, just before serving, the lobster meat is reheated almost to a boil in the stock, and then set aside, for a few minutes, to finish cooking in the residual heat remaining in the hot poaching liquid. Avoid boiling the stock; it will toughen the lobster meat.

1 In a large stockpot, bring 3.4 litres (6 pints) of water to the boil. Add the lobsters and bring water back to a boil. Boil gently for 8 minutes; remove and set aside. When cool enough to handle, remove the meat from the shells (reserving the shells from around the body) and set aside the tomalley and coral (about $1/2$ cup combined).

2 To concentrate the taste of the stock, reduce it to 4 cups. You will need 1 cup to reheat the lobster meat and $1/2$ cup for the sauce. Freeze the remainder.

For couscous:

1 Heat the 2 tablespoons of olive oil and sauté the onions over medium heat for about 2 minutes. Add the light green tomalley and dark green eggs and mix well, crushing the eggs with a fork. Stir in the couscous, and then add $1\,1/2$ cups boiling water, $1/2$ teaspoon salt and $1/4$ teaspoon pepper. Mix well. Remove from heat, cover; set aside for 10 minutes.

2 Combine the lobster meat with the 1 cup of reduced stock in a saucepan. Slowly bring stock almost to a boil and keep it at this temperature for 3 to 4 minutes, being careful that it does not boil.

For chive sauce:

1 Combine the stock, olive oil, chives, salt and pepper in a saucepan and bring to a strong boil.

2 Cut the reserved shells in half and fluff the couscous. Place some couscous on each plate and a shell receptacle on top. Fill the shell with couscous, arrange the warm lobster on top, and spoon sauce over to serve.

Trout on Ratatouille

FARMED trout are now available almost everywhere. Here, I coat the fish with an intensely flavoured tarragon oil, made by combining tarragon leaves, chives, water and a little olive oil together in a small food processor.

SERVES 4

Ratatouille

4 tablespoons virgin olive oil

1 medium onion, 100 g (4 oz), peeled and chopped

1 small aubergine, 175 g (6 oz), cut into 2 cm (3/4 in) pieces

1 small green pepper, cut into 1 cm (1/2 in) pieces

1 courgette, 175 g (6 oz), cut into 1 cm (1/2 in) pieces

1 large ripe tomato, halved, seeded and cut into 1 cm (1/2 in) pieces

4 cloves garlic, peeled, crushed and finely chopped

3/4 teaspoon salt

1/4 teaspoon freshly ground black pepper

Tarragon Oil

2 tablespoons (loose) fresh tarragon leaves

2 tablespoons fresh chives, snipped

3 tablespoons water

2 tablespoons virgin olive oil

4 trout fillets

1/4 teaspoon salt

For the ratatouille:

1 In a large frying pan or saucepan, heat the olive oil and sauté the onion in the hot oil for 2 minutes. Add the aubergine and sauté for 2 minutes, then add the green pepper and courgette and sauté for 1 minute longer. Stir in the tomatoes, garlic, salt, and pepper. Lower the heat, cover, and cook for 10 minutes. Set aside.

For the tarragon oil:

1 Meanwhile, place the tarragon, chives, water and olive oil in a food processor and process until liquified. Pour into a bowl. Set aside.

For the trout:

1 Place the trout, salt, and 1/4 cup water in a saucepan and bring to the boil. When boiling, reduce the heat, cover, and cook for 3 minutes on the first side. Then turn and cook for 3 minutes on the other side, or until tender.

2 To serve, divide the ratatouille between four plates and arrange a fish fillet on top of each portion. Coat lightly with the tarragon oil. Serve immediately.

Chicken and Seafood Paella

PAELLA is a complete meal. It contains a lot of rice flavoured with chorizo, the famed Spanish hot sausage; chicken legs; a seafood assortment of mussels, squid, and prawns; and finally, fresh vegetables. All of this is flavoured, of course, with pistils from the crocus flower – what we call saffron – the best quality of which comes from Spain. This one-pot meal requires great attention to timing. First, the pork and sausages are browned, and then, in their drippings, the chicken is browned. The rice is added next and cooked with the seasonings, and then the seafood is added. Finally, the asparagus and peas are placed in the pot. By staggering the ingredient additions in this way, everything finishes cooking at the same time.

SERVES 6-8

75 g (3 oz) pancetta (best choice) or salt pork, cut into 5 mm (1/4 in) lardons

225 g (8 oz) chorizo (Spanish hot sausage), cut into 2.5 cm (1 in) pieces

3 tablespoons virgin olive oil

3 chicken legs, about 450 g (1 lb), skinned, carcass bone removed, and cut in half to separate thighs and drumsticks

1 medium onion, 175 g (6 oz), peeled and cut into 1 cm (1/2 in) pieces

5 cloves garlic, peeled, crushed and finely chopped

2 cups long grain rice

1/2 cup, about 15 g (1/2 oz) dry mushroom pieces

1 teaspoon (loose) saffron pistils, crushed between your thumb and fingers

1 teaspoon herbes de Provence

4 cups water

1 tomato, 225 g (8 oz), cut into 1 cm (1/2 in) pieces

1 red pepper 175 g (6 oz), cut into 1 cm (1/2 in) pieces

1 tablespoon chopped Jalapeño or chilli pepper

1 teaspoon salt

1/2 teaspoon freshly ground black pepper

450 g (1 lb) (about 12) mussels

225 g (8 oz) squid cleaned and cut into 4 cm (1 1/2 in) pieces

12 prawns, about 225 g (8 oz), shelled

1/2 cup fresh shelled or frozen baby pease

6 asparagus spears cut into 2.5 cm (1 in) pieces

1 tablespoon chopped chives

1/2 teaspoon Tabasco sauce

1 In a large saucepan, sauté the pork lardons and chorizos in olive oil for 5 minutes, partially covered to avoid splattering. Add the chicken and brown for 10 minutes over low to medium heat. Add the onions and garlic, and continue cooking for about 30 seconds.

2 Add the rice to the pot and mix it in well. Then stir in the mushrooms, saffron, *herbes de Provence*, water, tomato, red and Jalapeño peppers, salt and pepper, and mix well. Bring to the boil, cover, reduce heat, and cook gently for 25 minutes.

3 Add the mussels, squid, and prawns. Cook for 8 minutes. Then stir in the peas and asparagus and continue cooking, covered, for another 5 minutes.

4 Sprinkle with chives and serve with Tabasco sauce on the side.

A Spanish Word

Paella comes from the Spanish word for the pan (usually a big iron or steel frying pan or saucepan) in which this classic concoction is cooked. In keeping with tradition, people in Spain still often prepare this dish outdoors over a wood fire, bringing their chicken from the market and plucking it and cooking it with sausages and rice. Essentially, paella is a big stew of rice flavoured with poultry, meat, seafood – whatever one can afford – with some vegetables added near the end of the cooking time.

Chicken Legs with Wine and Yams

THIS is one of those complete casserole dishes that makes a whole meal by itself. I use chicken legs for this dish because they stew better than chicken breasts, which tend to get stringy. Notice, however, that I remove the skin from the legs, which eliminates most of the fat. One chicken leg per person is sufficient when the legs are divided into thighs and drumsticks, especially since there are several vegetable garnishes as well.

SERVES 4

4 chicken legs, about 1.5 kg (3 lb) total

2 tablespoons virgin olive oil

1/4 cup chopped onion

4 large shallots, about 175 g (6 oz), peeled

8 medium mushrooms, about 150 g (5 oz)

4 yams, about 450 g (1 lb), peeled and halved lengthwise

1 cup dry white wine

8 large garlic cloves, peeled

1/2 teaspoon salt

1/2 teaspoon freshly ground black pepper

2 tablespoons chopped parsley, for garnish

1 Remove the skin from the chicken legs, using kitchen paper to help pull it off. In some supermarkets, chicken legs are packed with a piece of back carcass attached to the joint of the pelvis. If this is the case, remove any attached carcass bones from the chicken legs and then separate the legs into thighs and drumsticks.

2 Heat the olive oil in one large or two smaller frying pans and brown the chicken pieces (partially covered to prevent splattering) on all sides for about 10 minutes.

3 Add the onion and cook for 1 minute, then add the shallots, mushrooms, yams, wine, garlic, salt and pepper.

4 Bring to the boil, cover, and boil very gently for 20 minutes. Garnish with parsley and serve.

Chicken in Tarragon Sauce

THIS is an elegant dish that you can make easily and quickly if you buy skinless chicken breasts from the supermarket. I add some cream at the end here, and garnish the dish with fresh tarragon, which goes particularly well with the chicken and cream.

SERVES 4

6 pieces of skinless chicken (2 drumsticks and 2 thighs with bones left in, and 2 boneless breasts)

1/2 cup dry, fruity white wine

1 small onion, about 75 g (3 oz), chopped

1/2 cup good quality chicken stock, preferably home-made (see Chicken Broth, page 31)

2 bay leaves

1 sprig fresh thyme

1/2 teaspoon salt

1/4 teaspoon freshly ground black pepper

1 teaspoon potato flour or plain flour dissolved in 1 tablespoon water

1/4 cup double cream

1 teaspoon chopped fresh tarragon, for garnish

1 Place the chicken drumsticks, thighs, wine, onion, stock, bay leaves, thyme, salt and pepper in a saucepan, and bring to the boil. Reduce the heat, cover and boil gently for about 10 minutes.

2 Add the breast meat, cover and boil gently for another 10 minutes.

3 Transfer the meat to a dish and keep warm. Measure the cooking liquid. There should be about 1 cup; if there is more, reduce it to 1 cup.

4 Stir in the dissolved potato flour, bring to the boil, and then add the cream and return to the boil. Return the chicken pieces to the pan and heat them through. Remove from the heat, sprinkle with the tarragon and serve.

TIMING TIP

Notice that the dark meat is cooked for about 20 minutes and the breast meat is cooked for only 10 minutes. Delaying the addition of the white meat prevents it from becoming overcooked, which makes it stringy.

Grilled Chicken with Cabbage Anchoïade

IN this recipe, the chicken breasts are marinated for several hours in a finely chopped mixture of oregano, lemon skin, black pepper, and olive oil. Cooked on a hot grill, the breasts will brown quickly and remain moist in the centre.

SERVES 4

8 strips lemon peel, removed with a vegetable peeler

2 teaspoons black peppercorns

4 tablespoons fresh oregano

4 boneless skinless chicken breasts, about 225 g (8 oz) each, from roasting chickens

3 tablespoons virgin olive oil

1 teaspoon salt

Cabbage Anchoïade

4 cloves garlic, peeled, crushed and finely chopped

6 anchovy fillets, chopped fine

1/2 teaspoon salt

1/2 teaspoon freshly ground black pepper

1/2 red pepper, peeled and cut into 5 mm (1/4 in) dice

4 teaspoons red wine vinegar

4 tablespoons virgin olive oil

510 g (1 lb 2 oz) Savoy cabbage, shredded

1 Place the lemon strips, peppercorns and oregano in the bowl of a mini-chop, and process to a powder (about 4 tbsp). Sprinkle the mixture over the chicken and arrange it in a dish. Sprinkle with the olive oil. Cover, and set aside in the refrigerator to marinate for at least 30 minutes or as long as overnight.

2 At cooking time, sprinkle the chicken with salt and arrange it on a hot grill. Cook about 4 minutes on each side, and transfer to a warm oven, gas mark 4 350°F (180°C) until serving time (up to 1 hour ahead).

For cabbage anchoïade:

1 In a bowl, combine garlic, anchovies, salt, pepper, red pepper (reserving 1 tablespoon for garnish), vinegar and oil. Add the cabbage and mix well.

2 At serving time, arrange the cabbage mixture in a mound in the centre of four serving plates. Slice the chicken breasts lengthwise and arrange the meat all around and on top of the cabbage. Sprinkle with reserved red pepper and serve.

Poule au Pot

POULE is actually the French name for 'hen', and this famous 'chicken in a pot' dish originated in the sixteenth century under the rule of Henry IV. Conventionally, it is not as refined as I make it here by removing the meat from the bones and making the stock fat-free. Notice that everything is used, including the stock in which the chicken is cooked, so there is no loss of nutrients or vitamins.

SERVES 4-6

1 chicken, about 1.5 kg (3½ lbs)
1 teaspoon dried thyme leaves
1 teaspoon dried rosemary
3 bay leaves
12 cloves
2 teaspoons salt
1 teaspoon black peppercorns

Vegetables
2 large leeks, about 350 g (12 oz), cleaned
4 medium onions, 275 g (10 oz) total, peeled
4 carrots, about 450 g (1 lb), peeled
1 small butternut squash, 450 g (1 lb), peeled, seeded and quartered
1 small Savoy cabbage, about 450 g (1 lb) quartered
4 large mushrooms, about 100g (4 oz)
16 slices, 50 g (2 oz), from a baguette, toasted in the oven
½ cup grated Gruyère cheese
Gherkins and hot mustard

A WORD ABOUT STOCK
The stock is strained through kitchen paper to eliminate as much fat as possible, but if time permits, it's a good idea to chill it and remove and discard additional fat that solidifies on top.

1 Place the chicken, breast side down, with the neck and heart in a narrow stainless steel stock pot. (Reserve the liver to sauté or freeze for future use.) Add 4.5 litres (8 pints) of water, and bring it to the boil over high heat. Reduce heat and boil gently for 10 minutes. Skim the cooking liquid to remove fat and impurities that come to the surface.

2 Add the thyme, rosemary, bay leaves, cloves, salt, and peppercorns to the stock. Cover and continue boiling gently for 25 minutes (for a total of 35 minutes). Remove the chicken from the pot. When it is cool enough to handle, pull off and discard the skin. Pull meat from bones, keeping it in the largest possible pieces. Set meat aside, covered, in about 1/2 cup of the stock. Place bones back in the remaining stock and boil gently for another hour.

3 Strain stock twice through a strainer lined with kitchen paper. Rinse out the pot and return the stock to the pot. You should have 8–9 cups. (If necessary, adjust with water.)

For vegetables:

1 Add leeks, onions, carrots, squash and cabbage to stock, and bring to the boil. Boil, covered, for 15 minutes. Add mushrooms and cook for another 5 minutes.

2 Reheat the meat and surrounding liquid and arrange it in the centre of a large platter. Remove the vegetables with a slotted spoon and arrange them around the chicken. Ladle some of the stock into small bowls and serve it with the croûtons and cheese; pass around gherkins and hot mustard at the table.

Poulet au Vin Rouge

THIS is a modern version of the classic *Coq au Vin* - rich in flavour but lower in calories than the original, and much faster to make. I divide the chicken into pieces, remove the skin, brown it, and cook it in red wine, adding the breast pieces at the end so they don't overcook. The onions are glazed separately in a little olive oil and sugar, with the mushrooms added near the end of the cooking time. Finally, everything is combined together and served with croûtons.

SERVES 4

1 chicken, 1.5-1.75 kg ($3^1/_2$-4 lb)

12 small button onions, 175 g (6 oz), peeled

2 tablespoons virgin oilve oil

$^1/_2$ cup water

$^1/_2$ teaspoon sugar

4 large mushrooms, 100 g (4 oz), quartered

$^1/_3$ cup finely chopped onion

3 cloves garlic, peeled, crushed and finely chopped

$1^1/_4$ cups dry, fruity red wine

$^1/_2$ teaspoon dried thyme leaves or 1 sprig fresh thyme

2 bay leaves

$^3/_4$ teaspoon salt

$^3/_4$ teaspoon freshly ground black pepper

1 teaspoon potato flour or plain flour dissolved in 2 tablespoons red wine

Croûtons

1 teaspoon corn oil

4 slices white bread

2 tablespoons chopped parsley

1 Cut the chicken into 4 pieces (2 breasts with wings and 2 legs). Cut off the wings and divide them at the joints into 3 pieces. Skin and bone the breasts. Set the breasts aside with the two meatier wing pieces. (Freeze the bones and wing tips for future use.) Skin the legs and separate the thighs from the drumsticks by

A MODERN VERSION

Poulet au Vin Rouge is a classic *coq au vin*, although historically the 'cock' – an older chicken – was so tough that it had to be cooked for a long time and then the juices were thickened with the blood of the chicken. Now, with the tender chickens we have available, this dish can be made quickly. The skin of the chicken is removed and the meat cooked in red wine. Happily, more than 50 per cent of the wine's calories disappear through the cooking process.

cutting through them at the joint. Cut the ends off the drumsticks. The thigh and drum bones should be left in. Set the legs aside with the breasts and reserved wing pieces.

2 Place the button onions with 1 tablespoon of the olive oil, the sugar, and 1/2 cup water in a large saucepan, and bring to the boil over high heat. Boil for a few minutes, or until the water has evaporated and the onions start frying. Cook until the onions are browned on all sides. Add the mushrooms and sauté for 1 minute. Set aside, covered.

3 In a large frying pan, heat the remaining 1 tablespoon olive oil. When hot, sauté the chicken wing pieces for 2 to 3 minutes, until lightly browned on all sides. Add the leg pieces and brown them for about 2 to 3 minutes on each side. Repeat with the breasts. Set all the chicken pieces aside.

4 To the drippings in the frying pan, add the chopped onions and sauté them for 1 minute, then add the garlic and cook for about 10 seconds. Add the wine, thyme, bay leaves, salt, and pepper, and bring to a boil. Return the dark meat and the wings to the pan, cover, and boil very gently for 8 minutes.

5 Add the chicken breasts, and boil gently for another 7 minutes. This brings the total cooking time to 15 minutes for the dark meat, and only 7 minutes for the breast meat.

6 Add the dissolved potato flour to the pan and stir until the pan juices are thickened, then add the button onions and mushrooms with their juices to the red wine sauce.

For croûtons:

1 Trim the crusts from the bread, and cut the slices diagonally into triangles. Trim each triangle to form a heart-shaped croûton.

2 Spread the teaspoon of oil on a baking sheet and press the croûtons into the oil so they are moistened on both sides. Place in an oven heated to gas mark 6, 400°F (200°C) for 8–10 minutes, until nicely browned.

3 To serve, cut the chicken breasts in half and serve one piece of breast, one piece of drum or thigh meat, and one piece of wing per person with two croûtons, first dipping the tip of each croûton into the sauce to moisten it, and then into the chopped parsley. Sprinkle the remaining chopped parsley over the chicken.

Brown Rice Chicken Fricassee

FOR this fricassee, I use short grain brown rice, which takes about an hour to cook. To reduce the cooking time by 15 minutes, substitute medium grain white rice. Only the wing pieces have skin on them, but these render enough fat to brown the rest of the bones. Use a sturdy frying pan to cook the bones long enough so that they are nicely browned.

SERVES 4

About 750 g (1¾ lb) chicken bones, including neck, gizzard, and wing sections

1 large onion, 175 g (6 oz), peeled and coarsely chopped (1¼ cups)

1½ cups short grain brown rice

1 ripe tomato, chopped or 1 cup drained canned tomato, crushed

2-3 cloves garlic, peeled, crushed and finely chopped

1 small Jalapeño or chilli pepper, seeded and chopped

¼ cup coarsely chopped fresh coriander with stems

1 teaspoon salt

¼ teaspoon freshly ground black pepper

¾ cup olives, cut int 1 cm (½ in) pieces

⅓ cup dark raisins

3 cups water

1 In a large saucepan, sauté the chicken bones over medium to high heat for 15 minutes until nicely browned.

2 Add the onions and sauté for 1 minute, then stir in the rice.

3 Add the tomatoes, garlic, Jalapeño pepper, coriander, salt, pepper, olives, raisins, and water and bring the mixture to the boil. Reduce the heat, cover, and boil gently for 50 minutes.

4 Remove the bones, and when cold enough to handle, pick the meat from them and return it to the dish. Serve.

CLAUDINE'S FRICASSEE

My daughter, Claudine, has a favourite chicken fricassee dish, too. In her version, cooked chicken gizzards are combined with the same rice, garlic and onion that I use but she flavours her fricassee with coriander and extends it with courgettes and aubergine.

Grilled Quail on Quinoa with Sunflower Seeds

QUINOA, a grain that dates back to the Incas, is one of the super grains of the future, high not only in fibre but in Vitamins A and B and phosphorous. As quinoa cooks, it becomes almost transparent. I have added sautéed sunflower seed and dried currants to this recipe that features grilled boneless quail. Fish sauce is available from Chinese supermarkets.

SERVES 4

Marinade

1 medium-size shallot, peeled

1 large clove garlic, peeled

1 tablespoon fish sauce (nuoc-mam)

½ teaspoon sugar

¼ small Jalapeño or chilli pepper

1 tablespoon water

4 boneless quail, about 100 g (4 oz) each

Quinoa

2 tablespoons groundnut oil

1 small onion, chopped (about ½ cup)

2 tablespoons sunflower (or pumpkin) seeds, hulled

2 tablespoons dried currants

175 g (6 oz) quinoa

1¾ cups chicken stock, preferably home-made (see Chicken Broth, page 31)

¾ teaspoon salt

¼ teaspoon freshly ground black pepper

1 Place the shallots, garlic, fish sauce, sugar, Jalapeño pepper and water in a small mini-chop or food processor, and process until liquified. Place the quail in a flat dish and pour over the marinade, turning until coated. Cover and refrigerate for at least one hour.

2 At cooking time, place the quail on a very hot grill and cook for 2½–3 minutes on each side. Transfer to a dish and keep warm in an oven heated to gas mark 4, 350°F (180°C) until serving time (up to 45 minutes).

For quinoa:

1 Heat the oil in a frying pan and when hot, sauté the onions and seeds for 2 minutes.

2 Add the currants and quinoa and mix well. Stir in the stock, salt and pepper. Bring to a boil, reduce the heat, cover, and boil gently for about 18 minutes, until fluffy and tender.

For grilling quail:

1 Place quail on very hot grill and cook for 2-3 minutes on each side. Transfer to a dish and keep warm in the oven.

2 Arrange quinoa in the centre of individual plates and place a quail on top. Pour any natural juices that have accumulated in the dish over the quail.

Roasted Turkey with Mushroom Stuffing

ON holidays, I like to serve a small roasted turkey with whole wheat stuffing flavoured with golden raisins and dried mushrooms, which have a highly concentrated taste. Be sure to use the soaking liquid from the mushrooms to moisten the stuffing. Begin by roasting the turkey, breast-side-up at a high temperature for about 30 minutes, or until the skin is brown and crispy. Turn the turkey over, reduce the heat, and continue roasting it upside-down (so that the juices flow through the breasts). Near the end of cooking time, invert the turkey again, to re-brown the breast skin.

SERVES 8–10

1 5 kg (11 lb) turkey

1/2 teaspoon salt

1/2 teaspoon freshly ground black pepper

3 onions, about 350 g (12 oz), peeled and cut into 2.5 cm (1 in) dice

10 cloves garlic, unpeeled

1 teaspoon potato flour dissolved in 1 tablespoon water

1 tablespoon soy sauce

Stuffing

3/4 cup diced mushroom pieces, preferably cèpes, about 20 g (3/4 oz)

1 1/2 cups warm water, for soaking mushrooms

2 tablespoons virgin olive oil

2 tablespoons corn oil

1 medium onion, 175 g (6 oz), peeled and chopped fine

1-2 stalks celery (white, from inside), chopped (1/2 cup)

1/2 teaspoon herbes de Provence

3 cloves garlic, peeled, crushed and finely chopped

6 slices, about 200 g (7 oz) sprouted wheat bread (wholewheat bread made with wheat kernels)

1/3 cup golden raisins

1/2 teaspoon salt

1/4 teaspoon freshly ground black pepper

For turkey:

1 Reserve the turkey liver for another use and place the neck, gizzard, and heart in a saucepan with 2 cups of water. Bring to a boil, cover, reduce the heat, and cook over a low heat for about 1 hour. Drain, reserving the cooking liquids and the solids separately. You should have about 1½ cups of cooking liquid. Set aside. Pull the meat from the neck bones and cut it with the gizzard and heart into 5 mm (¼ in) dice. Place in a bowl and reserve.

2 Pre-heat the oven to gas mark 7, 425°F (220°C). Sprinkle the turkey inside and out with the salt and pepper and place it breast-side-up in a large roasting pan. Bake for 30 minutes.

3 Turn the turkey so it is breast-side-down. Arrange the onions and garlic cloves around it. Reduce the oven temperature to gas mark 4, 350°F (180°C). Return turkey to the oven and cook for 1½ hours, then add the 1½ cups reserved cooking liquid (from the neck, gizzard, and heart), turn the turkey so it is breast-side-up, and continue cooking it for another 30 minutes to brown the breast. Turn the oven off, transfer the turkey to an ovenproof platter, and return it to the warm oven to rest.

For stuffing:

1 Pre-heat the oven to gas mark 6, 400°F (200°C).

2 Place the mushrooms in a bowl and add the water. Set aside for at least 30 minutes. Drain, press (reserving the soaking liquid in the bowl), and coarsely chop the mushrooms, and set them aside with the soaking liquid.

3 Heat the oils in a large frying pan or saucepan. When hot, saute the onions and celery for 3 minutes. Add the *herbes de Provence*, garlic, and mushrooms, mix well, and remove from the heat. Toast the bread slices well, and cut them into 1 cm (⅜ in) croûtons. (You should have 3 cups.) Stir the croûtons and raisins into the mixture in the frying pan.

4 Pour the reserved mushroom soaking liquid into a measuring cup, leaving behind and discarding the sandy residue in the bottom of the bowl. (You should have about ¾ cup.)

5 Add to the mixture in the frying pan with the salt and pepper, and toss gently to combine. Pack lightly into a loaf pan and cover with aluminum foil. Bake in the pre-heated oven for 30 minutes.

For gravy:

1 Push the vegetables and cooking juices from the roasting pan through a sieve or a food mill (if you want to include the puréed vegetables in your gravy) into a saucepan.

2 Let rest for 4-5 minutes, until most of the fat has risen to the top, and skim off as much as possible. You should have about 2 cups of cooking juices.

3 Add the reserved diced neck, gizzard, and heart meat, and simmer the mixture for 10 minutes to reduce it slightly. Stir in the dissolved potato flour and soy sauce until smooth.

4 Carve the turkey and serve it with the gravy and mushroom stuffing.

Ragout of Rabbit

THIS recipe exemplifies the earthy country cooking of France. After dry roasting the rabbit in a large frying pan for about 30 minutes, until it is almost cooked, I make an appealing sauce with the solidified pan juices, garlic, onions, tomatoes and a reduction of vinegar.

SERVES 4

1 tablespoon unsalted butter
2 tablespoons virgin olive oil
1 young rabbit, about 1.25 kg ($2^1/_2$ lb), cut into 10-12 pieces
$^3/_4$ teaspoon salt
$^3/_4$ teaspoon freshly ground black pepper
5-6 cloves garlic, peeled, crushed and chopped
2 onions, 175 g (6 oz), peeled and chopped
$^1/_4$ cup red wine vinegar
1 ripe tomato, coarsely chopped (1 cup)
1 tablespoon chopped chives, for garnish

1 Heat the butter and oil in a 30 cm (12 in) frying pan. Season the rabbit pieces with $^1/_2$ teaspoon each of the salt and pepper.

2 Arrange rabbit pieces in the pan and brown them, covered, over a medium to high heat for 40 minutes, turning them every 10 minutes. (Add a few tablespoons of water if the pan becomes so dry that the rabbit starts burning.) The rabbit exterior should be crusty and brown and the juices well crystallized.

3 Transfer the rabbit to a dish, and add the garlic and onions to the juices in the pan. Sauté for 2-3 minutes, then add the vinegar and cook, stirring to dissolve the solidified juices, for about 2 minutes or until the mixture is reduced to a glaze.

4 Add the tomatoes and remaining salt and pepper. Return the rabbit to the sauce and heat gently for 2-3 minutes. Sprinkle with chives and serve immediately.

Veal Chops with Mushrooms

I USE relatively small veal chops here, each weighing about 225 g (8 oz) with the bone. Veal is low in calories and most supermarkets offer a good quality, milk-fed variety. If you can, buy it occasionally, as I do, from farms that feed their cows organic foods. The quality is dramatically better. The mushrooms are sautéed in the veal drippings, creating a delicious sauce for serving on the chops.

SERVES 4

2 teaspoons virgin olive oil
2 teaspoons unsalted butter
4 veal loin chops, about 2 cm (3/4 in) thick, 225 g (8 oz) each, preferably white milk-fed veal
1/2 teaspoon salt
1/2 teaspoon freshly ground black pepper
2 shallots, peeled and chopped
350 g (12 oz) mushrooms, sliced (about 5 cups)
1/4 cup dry white wine
2 cloves garlic, peeled, crushed and finely chopped
1/4 cup chopped parsley

1 Heat the oil and butter in a large frying pan. Sprinkle the veal chops with half the salt and pepper, and sauté in the hot oil and butter for 4 minutes on each side. Remove to a platter.

2 In the pan drippings, sauté the shallots for 10 seconds over medium heat. Add the mushrooms and wine, and cook, covered, for 1 minute.

3 Then uncover and cook for another minute. Add the garlic and remaining salt and pepper. Toss and cook for 10 seconds, then stir in the parsley. Pour the mushroom sauce over the veal chops. Serve immediately.

Roast of Veal with Artichokes

A PIECE of shoulder is the best choice for this recipe. Sometimes, if you buy the large muscle of the shoulder, you don't have to tie the meat; if, however, the piece is separating or is longer and flatter, it should be rolled and tied with string. This roast is good served cold with a green salad, tomato salad or pasta salad.

SERVES 4

1.25 kg (2½ lb) boneless veal shoulder roast, trimmed of most surface fat (Note: my roast was about 22 cm (8½ in) long by 6.5 cm (2½ in) in diameter.)

½ teaspoon salt

½ teaspoon freshly ground black pepper

1 teaspoon dried thyme leaves

1 tablespoon unsalted butter

1 tablespoon virgin olive oil

5 medium artichokes, with stems, about 750 g (1¾ lb)

12 onions, 400 g (14 oz), each about the size of a ping-pong ball, peeled

18 large cloves garlic, peeled

1 tomato, 175 g (6 oz), cut in half, seeded, and cut into 1 cm (½ in) pieces

1 tablespoon soy sauce

2 tablespoons water

1 Tie the trimmed roast with string if necessary and sprinkle it with ¼ teaspoon each of the salt and pepper, and the thyme. In an ovenproof frying pan heat the butter and oil. When hot, add the meat, and brown it on all sides for a total of 8 to 10 minutes. Remove the roast to a platter and reserve the drippings.

2 With a sharp knife, remove the top third of the artichokes. Then, trim off the upper half of remaining leaves with scissors to remove the thorny projections. Cut the artichokes into quarters and remove and discard the chokes.

3 Heat the oven to gas mark 6, 400°F (200°C). Add the artichokes, onions, garlic and remaining salt and pepper to the drippings in the frying pan and toss the vegetables to coat them with the drippings. Arrange the roast on top of the vegetables and place the pan in the oven for 20 minutes. Turn the roast over, stirring the vegetables as you do so, and return the pan to the oven for another 20 minutes. Stir in the tomatoes, soy sauce and water, and cook for an additional 10 minutes, for a total cooking time of 1 hour (not including browning).*

4 Remove the roast from the oven and allow it to rest for 10 minutes before carving and serving.

* Note: If your roast is shorter and thicker than mine (see ingredients list), cook it a little longer.

Wine Merchant Steak

THE steaks in this classic bistro dish are relatively small compared to those served a few years ago. In addition, they are trimmed of all fat, leaving them with a weight of about 200 g (7 oz) each, an ample serving. Although the steaks can be grilled and served plain, I extend the dish with a sauce made of shallots, mushrooms, garlic, and a good, earthy wine, thickened with Dijon mustard, and garnished with chopped chives.

SERVES 4

4 Sirloin steaks 250 g (9 oz) each, about 2 cm (3/4 in) thick

3/4 teaspoon salt

1/2 teaspoon freshly ground black pepper

2 tablespoons virgin olive oil

2 shallots, peeled and chopped fine

4 large mushrooms, about 100g (4 oz), julienned

2 large cloves garlic, peeled, crushed and finely chopped

1 cup red wine (Beaujolais-type)

1 cup chicken broth, preferably home-made (see Chicken Broth, page 00)

1 tablespoon Worcestershire sauce

1 tablespoon Dijon mustard

1/2 teaspoon arrowroot mixed with 2 teaspoons water

1 tablespoon finely chopped fresh chives

1 Trim the steaks, removing all visible surface fat and sinews. The trimmed steaks should weigh about 200 g (7 oz) each.

2 Sprinkle the steaks with 1/2 teaspoon of the salt and the pepper.

3 Heat the olive oil in a large frying pan; when hot, add the steaks and sauté for 2 1/2 minutes on each side for medium rare.

4 Remove the steaks to a plate and set aside in a warm place. To the drippings in the frying pan, add the shallots and sauté for about 10 seconds. Add

the mushrooms and garlic, and sauté for 1 minute. Stir in the wine, and boil it down until only about 2 tablespoons remain. Add the stock, and reduce the mixture to about 3/4 cup.

5 Add the Worcestershire sauce, mustard, and remaining salt, and mix well. Stir in the arrowroot and bring the mixture to the boil.

6 Arrange the steaks on individual plates and spoon some sauce on top and around each steak. Garnish with the chives and serve.

Spicy Beef Roast

If you allow only a small portion of meat per serving, and trim it completely, beef is a perfectly acceptable component of well-balanced diet. It is, in fact, a good source of iron. Moreover, using dry herbs, as I do here to flavour the meat, enables me to cut back on the amount of salt I use. Notice that the beef is cooked initially on top of the stove before it is finished in the oven; this produces an exterior crust that intensifies the taste of the meat.

SERVES 4

1 sirloin of beef, about 750 g (1 1/2 lb)
1 teaspoon dried thyme
1 teaspoon dried oregano
1 teaspoon dried rosemary
1/4 teaspoon freshly ground black pepper
1/4 teaspoon cayenne pepper
1/4 teaspoon salt
1 tablespoon virgin olive oil
1/4 cup chicken stock

1 Remove all surface fat from the roast. The trimmed roast should weigh 550 g (1 1/4 lb) and be 4.5 cm (1 3/4 in) thick.

2 Crush the dried herbs between your thumb and finger, and mix them with the black and cayenne peppers. Pat the mixture on both sides of the meat.

3 Pre-heat the oven to gas mark 8, 450°F (230°C). Sprinkle the roast with the salt. Heat the oil in a heavy ovenproof frying pan or saucepan. When hot, add the meat and cook over medium to high heat for 3 minutes on each side.

4 Then transfer the roast to the pre-heated oven and cook for 8–10 minutes for medium to rare. Add the chicken stock and let rest 10 minutes before carving. Serve with the natural meat cooking juices.

Grilled Lamb Chops with Savory

THESE are best cooked on a very hot grill, so turn on the grill early enough so that it is generating a lot of heat when you are ready to cook. Without the bone, these chops would each weigh only about 100 g (4 oz), which is adequate when they are served with vegetables or other dishes.

SERVES 4

4 lamb chops, about 4 cm (1½ in) thick 175 g (6 oz) each, well trimmed
¼ teaspoon freshly ground black pepper
2 tablespoons chopped fresh savory
1 tablespoon virgin olive oil
½ teaspoon salt

1 Sprinkle the chops on both sides with the pepper and the savory.

2 Pour the olive oil onto a plate and dip the chops, one side and then the other, in the oil.

3 Arrange the chops on the plate, cover with plastic wrap, and refrigerate until ready to cook later that day.

4 At cooking time, sprinkle the chops with salt. Cook over high heat on a grill for about 3½–4 minutes on each side for medium rare meat.

5 Transfer to a warm oven and allow the chops to rest for a few minutes before serving.

A WORD ABOUT LAMB CHOPS

Loin chops are readily available at supermarkets. They have a small T-bone in them and are more meaty than rib lamb chops. Trim off any large pieces of outside fat, sprinkle with the seasonings and oil, and either cook them immediately or allow them to marinate, refrigerated, until cooking time.

Irish Lamb Stew

IN this recipe, the vegetable garnishes are cooked separately in water, and then that water, which contains all the vegetables' nutrients, is used to cook the lamb. The trimmings from these vegetables are added to the stew and become the thickening agent for a gravy made from the natural cooking juices. This makes for a flavoursome and hearty dish that is also low in calories and fat.

SERVES 6

750 g (1 1/2 lb) potatoes

3 carrots, about 275 g (10 oz)

3-4 sticks of celery, about 150 g (5 oz)

750 g (1 1/2 lb) lamb from the leg or shoulder, well trimmed and cut into 2.5 cm (1 in) cubes

2 medium onions, about 225 g (8 oz), peeled and quartered

3 large cloves garlic, peeled

3 sprigs fresh thyme or 1 teaspoon dried tyme

2 bay leaves

1/2 teaspoon freshly ground black pepper

2 teaspoons Worcestershire sauce

1 tablespoon chopped parsley

1 Peel the potatoes and cut them into 18 pieces of about equal size. Round off the cut corners of each potato piece and reserve the trimmings. You should have about 2 cups of trimmings and 18 small, 'roundish' potatoes, all approximately the same size. Peel the carrots and cut them into sticks 4.5 cm (1 3/4 in) long by 1 cm (1/2 in) thick. Trim the celery sticks (reserving the trimmings) and cut them into sticks 5 cm (2 in) long by 1 cm (1/2 in) wide.

2 Place the potatoes in a saucepan and add 3 cups of water. Bring to a boil, reduce the heat, and boil gently, covered, for 12 minutes. Drain, reserving the cooking liquid, and set the potatoes aside. Return the reserved cooking liquid to the saucepan, add the carrots and celery, and bring back to the boil. Boil gently for 5 minutes. Drain, reserving the cooking liquid. (You should have about 2 cups of liquid; adjust with water as needed.)

3 Place the lamb in a dutch oven or cooking pot with a tight-fitting lid and add the reserved cooking liquid and the potato and celery trimmings. Then, stir in the onions, garlic, thyme, bay leaves, salt, pepper and Worcestershire sauce, and bring to the boil. Reduce heat, cover and boil gently for 45 minutes.

4 Remove the meat, push the cooking juices and vegetable pieces through a food mill (or process momentarily in a food processor), and place them back in the pot with the meat. Add the reserved small potatoes, celery and carrot sticks to the pot, and bring to the boil. Simmer 5 minutes. Sprinkle with parsley, and serve immediately.

Grilled Leg of Lamb

In this receipe, a mini-chop comes in handy to reduce the marinade ingredients to a purée. If you don't have a mini-chop, use a food processor or blender. The lamb can be marinated for up to a day or at least for a few hours before it is grilled. After grilling, the lamb is transferred to a warm oven, where it finishes cooking in its own residual heat.

SERVES 4

Marinade
24 mint leaves (about 1/3 cup, lightly packed)
1/2 small Jalapeño or chilli pepper
1 piece of ginger (about 1 tbs), peeled
2 cloves garlic, peeled
2 tablespoons apricot jam
1 tablespoon soy sauce
3 tablespoons water

750 g (1 1/2 lb) piece boneless lamb from the back leg, trimmed of most of the fat

1 Place the mint leaves, Jalapeño pepper, ginger, garlic, jam, soy sauce and water in the bowl of mini-chop, and process until liquified.

2 Transfer to a plastic bag. Place the lamb in the bag with the seasoning and seal the bag. Refrigerate for at least 2 hours or overnight to allow the meat to marinate in the seasonings

3 To cook, remove the lamb from the bag and dry it off with kitchen paper.

4 Place it on a grill under very high heat for about 7 minutes on each side. Then, transfer the meat to a roasting pan, pour the reserved marinade around it, and place it in a heated oven to gas mark 1/4, 200°F (95°C) for at least 15 minutes.

5 Slice and serve with some of the juices.

Saucisses au Chou on Lentils

IT is best to buy a lean piece of pork and grind it yourself for the sausage patties in this recipe. Highly seasoned with coriander, cumin, and hot pepper, the patties are wrapped in blanched Savoy cabbage leaves, so the meat stays juicy and moist as it cooks. If you don't have access to a grill, sauté six patties at a time in a non-stick pan, cooking them in 2 teaspoons of safflower oil for about 5 minutes on each side. In this recipe, lentils, very high in soluble fibre, are cooked with seasonings and then combined with a little olive oil, garlic, pepper, Tabasco, and mustard. These could be served on their own as a first course or as a meat accompaniment.

SERVES 6

Sausage Mixture

750 g (1 1/4 lb) lean ground pork

1 1/2 teaspoons salt

1/4 teaspoon freshly ground black pepper

3/4 teaspoon fennel seed

1/2 teaspoon ground coriander seeds

1/2 teaspoon ground cumin

1/8 teaspoon cayenne pepper

1/8 teaspoon ground allspice

1/2 cup coarsely chopped mushrooms, about 50 g (2 oz)

6 large outer leaves from a Savoy cabbage, about 275g (10 oz)

Lentils

225 g (8 oz) green lentils

3 cups water

2 small onions, 100 g (4 oz), peeled and chopped

4 large cloves garlic, peeled, crushed and finely chopped

2 bay leaves

3/4 teaspoon salt

1/4 cup virgin olive oil

1/4 teaspoon freshly ground black pepper

1/4 teaspoon Tabasco sauce

1 1/2 tablespoons Dijon mustard

1 tablespoon chopped parsley, or coriander.

For sausage patties:

1 Thoroughly mix the sausage ingredients together in a bowl and refrigerate, covered. (This should be done a minimum of 2 hours before cooking so the seasonings can flavour the meat well. If prepared one day ahead, reserve the mushrooms, which might darken and discolour the mixture, and mix them in just before forming the mixture into patties.)

2 In a large saucepan, bring 6 cups of water to a boil, add the cabbage leaves, and bring the water back to the boil.

3 Cook the cabbage for 5 minutes, until soft but still firm. Drain and refresh under cool water.

4 Cut each leaf on either side of the centre stem. Discard the stems (or add them to soup). Form the sausage mixture into patties about 40–50 g (1½–2 oz) each, and wrap each patty in a piece of cooked cabbage leaf. You should have 12 patties.

For lentils:

1 Wash the lentils under cool, running water and place them in a pot with the water, onions, 2 teaspoons of the chopped garlic, bay leaves and salt.

2 Bring to the boil, cover, and boil gently for 20–25 minutes. The lentils should be tender and a little wet; if there is an excess of liquid remaining, drain it off. (One cup of raw lentils will yield 3 cups of cooked lentils.)

3 Add the olive oil, remaining teaspoon of garlic, pepper, Tabasco and mustard, and mix well. Set aside.

To cook patties:

1 Place the patties on a hot, well cleaned grill and cook for about 5 minutes on each side. Or, if a grill is not available, sauté the patties in a non-stick frying pan over a medium heat for about 5 minutes on each side.

2 To serve, divide the lentils among six plates and arrange two sausage patties on each plate. Sprinkle with the chopped parsley and serve immediately.

Braised Pork Cocotte

IN the interests of good health, it is important that you select a lean roast for this recipe. Although fatty roasts tend to be more moist, a lean one will be full of flavour if it is cooked very slowly with its garnishes.

SERVES 6

1 lean pork loin roast, about 750 g (1½ lb)

4 cloves garlic, peeled and cut in half lengthwise

½ teaspoon salt

¼ teaspoon freshly ground black pepper

1 tablespoon virgin olive oil

1 large or 2 medium onions, 225 g (8 oz), peeled and quartered

3 carrots, 225 g (8 oz), peeled and cut into 2.5 cm (1 in) pieces

1 tablespoon chopped fresh ginger

1 tablespoon chopped Jalapeño or chilli pepper

½ cup dried tomatoes reconstituted in 1 cup water (see Roasted Aubergine Sandwiches, page 113)

1 Trim the pork roast of most of the surface fat and make eight random shallow slits in it. Push half a garlic clove in each of the slits. Sprinkle the roast with the salt and pepper.

2 Heat the oil in a cocotte (round or oval casserole dish) or heavy saucepan with lid. When hot, cook the pork for 10 minutes over high heat, turning the meat to brown it on all sides.

3 Add the onions, carrots, ginger, pepper and tomatoes, including the soaking water from the tomatoes.

4 Cover, reduce the heat to very, very low, and cook for about 1½ hours. The meat should be tender when pierced with a fork and there should be some juice surrounding it.

5 Serve two slices of the pork per person with the vegetable garnishes and juices.

Smoked Pork Roast with Mustard-Honey Glaze

GUESTS will love to help themselves to this mouthwatering glazed pork roast. Served with braised cabbage (page 93) and a simple salad, it makes a wonderful party menu.

SERVES 10

1 smoked pork shoulder, bone in, about 2.8 kg (6¼ lb)

Glaze
2 tablespoons honey
2 tablespoons dry mustard
½ teaspoon paprika
⅛ teaspoon cayenne pepper
½ cup water
1 tablespoon cider vinegar

1 Place the pork shoulder in a stock pot and cover it with enough cold water to extend 1 cm (¼ in) above the meat. Bring the water to 180°F (82°C) (this will take about 15 to 20 minutes) and cook at 180–190°C (82-88°C) for 1¼ hours. (Watch the temperature closely; the liquid should not boil.)

2 Meanwhile, in a small bowl mix together the honey, mustard, paprika and pepper. Set aside.

3 Let the pork cool in the cooking liquid, and then trim it, removing most of the exterior fat and rind from around the bones. Trim, also, the surface of the meat that is dark and leathery. Score the top of the ham every 2 cm (¾ in), and spread the glaze over the surface.

4 Pre-heat the oven to gas mark 5, 375°F (190°C). Place the ham in a roasting pan or saucepan and roast in the pre-heated oven for 1 hour. The surface should be nicely browned.

5 Transfer the meat to a serving platter, and add the water and vinegar to the drippings in the pan. Using a wooden spatula, scrape the bottom of the pan to dissolve any solidified cooking juices, and mix them with the water and vinegar. Strain the juices over the pork shoulder, and serve, slicing it at the table.

Accompaniments

Tomato, Onion and Parsley Vinaigrette
Broccoli Piquante
Braised Sour Cabbage
Peas à la Française
Cauliflower in Spring Onion Sauce
Corn and Pepper Sauté
Carotte Ciboulette
Purée of Carrot with Ginger
Curried Bulgar with Currants
Cornmeal au Gruyère
Pommes Anglaises
French Fries
Pommes Persillade
Turnips and Mashed Potatoes
Oeuf Cocotte
Mushroom Omelette
Rolls and Baguettes
Buttermilk Bread
Croque-Monsieur
James Beard's Onion Sandwiches
Smoked Salmon and Cucumber Sandwiches
Roasted Aubergine Sandwiches
Olive and Tomato Toasts
Pan Bagna
Jam 'Sandwiches'

Tomato, Onion and Parsley Vinaigrette

THIS is especially good when tomatoes – preferably organically grown ones – are at their peak. The seasonings are simple, consisting only of vinegar, oil, salt and pepper. If you don't have a red onion, you can use another mild variety of onion instead, and parsley can be replaced with basil, tarragon, or another herb to your liking.

SERVES 4

2 large ripe tomatoes, about 450 g (1lb)

1 medium red onion, about 75 g (3 oz)

1/4 teaspoon salt

1/4 teaspoon freshly ground black pepper

1 tablespoon red wine vinegar

3 tablespoons virgin olive oil

2 tablespoons chopped flat-leaf parsley

1 Cut the tomatoes into 5mm (1/4 in) slices and arrange the slices on a platter.

2 Peel the onion, cut it into very thin slices, and arrange on top of the tomato slices.

3 Sprinkle with salt, pepper, vinegar and oil.

4 At serving time, sprinkle with parsley and serve.

Broccoli Piquante

THE broccoli is steamed briefly so it keeps all its nutrients and its deep green colour. Flavoured with a simple sauce made of lemon juice, olive oil and Tabasco, this vegetable dish could be served as a first course.

SERVES 4

Sauce
1½ tablespoons lemon juice
2 tablespoons virgin olive oil
¼ teaspoon Tabasco sauce
¼ teaspoon salt

750 g (1½ lb) broccoli, washed

1 Combine the lemon juice, olive oil, Tabasco sauce and salt in a bowl. Mix well and set aside.

2 Separate the broccoli florets from the stems. Peel the stems, if the exterior is tough or fibrous, and cut them into slices about 5mm (½ in) thick by 5cm (2in) long.

3 Arrange the broccoli florets and stems on an ovenproof plate and place in a steamer (mine is bamboo). Steam, covered, over boiling water for 11–12 minutes.

4 Toss gently with the sauce and serve.

Braised Sour Cabbage

THE combination of sweet cider and cider vinegar gives this dish a sweet and sour taste that complements pork especially well, but also goes well with goose or duck. You can substitute red cabbage for Savoy cabbage and add some sliced apple, if you like.

SERVES 4

450 g (1lb) Savoy cabbage, cored and cut into 2.5 cm (1in) slices

1 medium onion, about175 g (6 oz), peeled and thinly sliced

3/4 cup dark raisins

1 cup sweet cider

3 tablespoons cider vinegar

3/4 teaspoon salt

1/4 teaspoon freshly ground black pepper

1/2 tablespoon corn oil

1 In a stainless steel saucepan, combine the cabbage, onion, raisins, cider, cider vinegar, salt, pepper and oil.

2 Bring to the boil, cover, reduce the heat to medium, and boil for 45 minutes. Most of the liquid should have evaporated by then, but the cabbage should be moist; cook for longer if there is excess moisture in the bottom of the pan. The small amount of liquid remaining in the pan should be caramelized and brown, and the cabbage a little crunchy. Serve.

Peas à la Française

THIS is a classic dish. Lettuce and tiny button onions are cooked first with a dash of oil and water, and then fresh shelled peas are added; the mixture is cooked some more. If fresh peas are not available, a packet of frozen baby peas will work quite well.

SERVES 4

225 g (8 oz) small pearl onions, (about 24)
1/2 teaspoon herbes de Provence
1 tablespoon sugar
1 teaspoon salt
1/4 teaspoon freshly ground black pepper
2 tablespoons virgin olive oil
1 cut water
1 small head lettuce, about 225 g (8 oz), rinsed well and cut into 5 cm (2 in) pieces
750 g (11/2 lb) fresh peas shelled, or 1 package 350 g (12 oz) frozen baby peas or petit pois
1 teaspoon arrowroot dissolved in 1 tablespoon water

1 In a saucepan combine the onions, *herbes de Provence*, sugar, salt, pepper, oil and water. Bring to the boil, reduce the heat, cover, and cook for 5 minutes. Add the lettuce and cook, covered, for about 3 to 5 minutes longer or until the lettuce has wilted. (The dish can be made ahead to this point.)

2 At serving time, add the peas to the lettuce mixture in the pan and bring to the boil. Boil for about 5 minutes if you are using fresh peas (adjusting as required based on the size of the peas), or 2 minutes if you are using frozen peas.

3 Mix in the dissolved arrowroot solution and bring the mixture back to the boil to thicken the juices. Serve as soon as possible.

Cauliflower in Spring Onion Sauce

CRISP, tender cauliflower florets are served with a tasty sauce of sautéed spring onions. Lightly browned breadcrumbs are sprinkled over the hot cauliflower at the last moment.

SERVES 4

1 head cauliflower about 550 g (1 1/4 lb), with green leaves removed
1 cup water
1 slice bread, toasted
3 tablespoons safflower oil
4 spring onions, finely chopped
1/4 teaspoon salt
1/4 teaspoon freshly ground black pepper

1 Separate the cauliflower into florets (making 14–16 pieces). In a large saucepan bring the water to the boil. Add the florets in one layer, cover and boil over high heat for about 8–10 minutes or until tender. (Most of the water should have evaporated.)

2 Meanwhile, break the toasted bread into the bowl of a food processor and process it until crumbed. (You should have about 3 tbsp.)

3 Heat the oil in a frying pan. When hot, add the spring onions and breadcrumbs and sauté over medium heat for about 1 1/2 minutes. Stir in the salt and pepper, and sprinkle the mixture over the hot cauliflower. Serve immediately.

PRESERVING NUTRIENTS
In this recipe, cauliflower florets are cooked in just enough water so that by the time the florets are tender, most of the water has evaporated and the nutrients and vitamins are preserved in the vegetable. If the dish is prepared ahead, reheat the cauliflower in a little water on the hob or in the oven.

Corn and Pepper Sauté

THIS is one of my favourite ways to prepare corn, high in Vitamins A and B, and red pepper, a good source of Vitamins A, B, C, and E. Fresh corn is sautéed very briefly in a frying pan and, since the starch in it doesn't cook long enough to set, the corn remains crunchy and sweet. It's an easy dish, especially good if the corn comes from an organic farm.

SERVES 4

2 ears fresh corn
1 large red pepper, 225 g (8 oz)
2 tablespoons unsalted butter
1/4 teaspoon salt
1/4 teaspoon freshly ground black pepper

1 Husk the ears of corn and cut off the kernels, to make about 2 cups. Set aside.

2 Using a vegetable peeler, remove as much of the skin as you can from the red pepper. (The firmer the pepper, the easier it is to peel.) Cut the pepper into sections, remove the seeds from each section and peel off any remaining skin. Cut the pepper into 5 mm (1/4 in) pieces). (You should have about 1 cup.)

3 Heat the butter in a frying pan. Add the corn and sauté in hot butter over high heat for about 2 minutes. Then add the red pepper, and sauté the mixture for 1 1/2 minutes longer. Stir in the salt and pepper, and serve immediately.

PEELING PEPPERS

I peel the red pepper with a vegetable peeler for this recipe, instead of placing it under the grill and peeling off the blistered skin, as is done conventionally. The vegetable remains quite firm and thick-walled when peeled. Use a good vegetable peeler and peel off as much of the skin from the whole vegetable as possible before cutting it into segments and removing additional skin from the recessed areas. Peeled pepper is quite sweet and is easily digested.

Carotte Ciboulette

THESE carrots are cooked in a little water along with butter and seasonings, but by the time they are cooked and tender, the water has evaporated, leaving all the nutrients and the concentrated taste of the seasoned carrots to enjoy.

SERVES 4

450 g (1lb) carrots, peeled and thinly sliced (about 3½ cups)
1 tablespoon unsalted butter
¾ cup water
1 teaspoon sugar
¾ teaspoon salt
¼ teaspoon freshly ground black pepper
2 tablespoons chopped chives, for garnish

1 Combine the carrots, butter, water, sugar, salt and pepper in a saucepan.

2 Bring to the boil, cover and cook for 5 minutes, until most of the moisture has evaporated and the carrots are just tender. (If there is an excess amount of liquid remaining in the pan, cook, uncovered, for a few minutes, or until most of the liquid had evaporated and the carrots start sizzling.)

3 Sprinkle with the chives and serve as soon as possible.

Purée of Carrot with Ginger

THE nutrient-rich water remaining in the saucepan after the carrots and ginger are cooked is added to the food processor to lend low-calorie moisture and flavour to the purée.

SERVES 4

750 g (1 1/2 lb) carrots, peeled
1 tablespoon root ginger, peeled and grated
3 cups water
2 tablespoons virgin olive oil
3/4 teaspoon salt
1/4 teaspoon freshly ground black pepper
1/4 cup milk

1 Cut the peeled carrots into 4 cm (1 1/2 in) chunks and place them in a saucepan. Add the ginger and water, and bring to the boil.

2 Cover the pan, reduce the heat and boil gently for 15 minutes, until tender. (Only about 1/2 cup of water should remain in the pan.)

3 Transfer the carrots and ginger with the cooking juices to the bowl of a food processor, and process for a few seconds and then add the remainder of the ingredients. Process until very smooth. Serve.

Curried Bulgar with Currants

BULGAR wheat – steamed, sun-dried and crushed wheat berries – is indigenous to Middle Eastern cooking. Like its uncooked relative, cracked wheat – another staple grain from that part of the world – it is high in protein, fibre, calcium, and potassium.

SERVES 4

1 tablespoon virgin olive oil
1 small onion, 50 g (2 oz) chopped
2 spring onions coarsely chopped
2 tablespoons currants
1 teaspoon curry power
1 cup bulgar wheat (available at health food stores)
2 cups chicken stock, preferably home-made (see Chicken Broth, page 31)
1/2 teaspoon salt

1 In a frying pan heat the olive oil. When hot, add the onions and spring onions, and sauté for 1 minute.

2 Stir in the currants and curry powder, then add the bulgar wheat, chicken stock, and salt. Mix well. Bring to a boil, cover, reduce the heat, and cook gently for 20 minutes. Fluff with a fork and serve immediately.

A WORD ABOUT BULGAR

You can make a salad with bulgar by simply reconstituting it in water and tossing it with vinegar, lemon juice and seasons – anything from spring onions to garlic. Here, I cook the bulgar with onions, flavour it with curry and mix in some currants. A filling, high-carbohydrate dish that is quick, easy and inexpensive to make, it goes particularly well with Grilled Lamb Chops with Savory (page 83).

Cornmeal au Gruyère

READY to eat in a few minutes, this fast polenta consists primarily of cornmeal and leeks, cooked together in a good chicken stock. If you want to lower the calories, serve this dish without the Gruyère cheese, although it adds texture and taste that go quite well with stews and roasted meat.

SERVES 4

2 1/4 cups chicken stock, preferably home-made (see Chicken Broth, page 31)

1 piece of leek, trimmed and finely chopped (1/2 cup)

1/2 teaspoon salt

1/4 teaspoon freshly ground black pepper

1/4 cup stone-ground yellow cornmeal

50 g (2 oz) Gruyère cheese, cut into 5 mm (1/4 in) dice

1 In a saucepan combine the stock, leek, salt and pepper, and bring the mixture to the boil. Whisk in the cornmeal and return to the boil.

2 Lower the heat, cover, and cook gently for 4 to 5 minutes, stirring occasionally.

3 Add the cheese and mix until it has melted into the mixture. Serve immediately.

Pommes Anglaises

THESE are simply steamed potatoes. It is important that you use potatoes of approximately the same size for this dish. If you can't find small, round, red-skinned potatoes, cut larger potatoes into equal size chunks and round off the corners to make them more uniformly shaped. Prepared at the last moment and eaten freshly steamed, these are moist and delicate, much more so than potatoes cooked and left standing in water.

SERVES 4

12 small new potatoes 750 g (1½ lb), peeled

1 Peel the potatoes and place them in a bowl of cold water until cooking time.

2 When ready to cook and serve, arrange them on an ovenproof plate and place in a steamer (mine is bamboo). Steam, covered, over boiling water for 26 minutes.

A LOW-CALORIE DINNER

For a complete low-calorie steamed dinner, serve the Pommes Anglaises with Salmon Pojarski (page 60) and Broccoli Piquante (page 92). I cook this menu in a three-tiered bamboo steamer, staggering the additions based on the cooking time required for each dish. I begin with the potatoes. Cover and steam them in one tier of the steamer over boiling water for 15 minutes. Then, a second tier containing broccoli is stacked on top, and the broccoli and potatoes steam, covered, for 5 additional minutes. Finally, the third tier is added, this one containing the salmon patties. Cover and steam all three tiers for an additional 6–7 minutes. Remove all three dishes from the steamer and serve together. Total steaming time for the meal is 26 minutes.

French Fries

THESE french fries are cooked as they are in professional kitchens. First they are blanched in oil that is not too hot, thus allowing them to cook without taking on any colour. This can be done hours ahead. Then, just before serving, they are browned quickly in very hot oil until crisp on the outside and soft and moist inside.

SERVES 4

3 large good quality potatoes, such as King Edward or Maris Piper, 1 kg (2 lb)
1½ cups vegetable oil
Salt, to taste

1 Peel the potatoes and cut them lengthwise into sticks 1cm (½ in) thick. Wash the sticks in cold water, drain, and pat dry.

2 In a 30 cm (12 in) non-stick frying pan, heat the oil to 175°C (350°F). Add the potatoes and cook for 5 minutes, until they are tender but still whitish. Remove and set aside until serving time. (You can prepare the recipe up to this point hours ahead).

3 At serving time, reheat the oil 200°C (400°F) and finish frying the potatoes, half at a time, for 4 to 5 minutes (shaking the pan occasionally to prevent them from sticking) until nicely browned and crisp.

4 Remove the potatoes from the oil, set them aside on absorbent kitchen paper, and repeat with the second batch. Sprinkle with salt and serve immediately.

A WORD ABOUT FRENCH FRIES

Notice that I start with 1½ cups of oil in this recipe. After the second cooking, you should have about 1¼ cups of oil remaining, meaning that the potatoes absorb only about ¼ cup of oil, or 1 tablespoon per portion. This is less oil than would have been used in the dressing if the potato had been made into a salad instead.

Pommes Persillade

THESE potatoes are a standard item on most bistro menus. Cut into little cubes, they can be sautéed in just a few minutes. They are best served immediately after cooking; if cooked ahead, they soften and lose the exterior crispness that contrasts so well with their soft interior.

SERVES 4

2 large potatoes, 510 g (18 oz) peeled
3 cloves garlic, peeled
1/4 cup loosely packed parsley leaves
2 tablespoon corn oil
1 teaspoon salt
1 teaspoon freshly ground black pepper

1 Cut the potatoes into 1 cm (3/8 in) cubes. Place in a sieve and rinse well under cool tap water. Place in a bowl with water to cover until ready to cook.

2 In a large non-stick frying pan, heat the oil. Drain the potatoes, pat dry with kitchen paper and add to the hot oil. Sauté over high heat for 12–14 minutes, stirring occasionally, until the potatoes are browned on all sides.

3 Meanwhile, chop the garlic and parsley together until finely minced and set the mixture aside. (This is a *persillade*). Add the salt, pepper and *persillade* to the potatoes in the pan, tossing to combine. Serve immediately.

POTATOES IN ADVANCE
The potatoes can be peeled and cut into cubes ahead, providing they are kept in water to cover so they don't discolour. Drain, dry with kitchen paper, and sauté quickly just before serving in a little corn oil, which can withstand high temperatures.

Turnips and Mashed Potatoes

IN this recipe potatoes and turnips are cooked in just enough water so that there is about 1/2 cup of liquid remaining in the pan when the vegetables are tender – enough to incorporate with them to create a nice purée. If a little more liquid is required, add a dash of water or stock; if there is too much liquid in the pan after the vegetables are cooked, remove the lid and quickly boil to reduce the liquid to 1/2 cup.

SERVES 4

3 large potatoes, 510 g (18 oz)
2 turnips, 175 g (6 oz) total
1 large clove garlic, peeled,
1/2 teaspoon salt
1 cup water
2 tablespoons unsalted butter

1 Peel the potatoes and turnips, and cut them into 5 cm (2 in) pieces.

2 Place in a saucepan with the garlic, salt and water. Bring to the boil, cover, reduce the heat, and boil gently for 20 minutes, until the vegetables are tender. There should be about 1/2 cup of liquid remaining. Adjust to this level, if necessary.

3 Transfer the mixture to the bowl of a food processor, add the butter and process until smooth and creamy. Serve.

A HINT ABOUT FLAVOUR
Although I don't use milk or cream, I do use a little butter. Select a good-quality butter and add it at the last moment for maximum taste advantage.

Oeuf Cocotte

THESE eggs are cooked in cocottes, which are little moulds that hold about $^1/_2$ cup. Although I use soufflé moulds, you can use any small, ovenproof moulds that are narrow enough so that an egg fills most of the container. The cocottes are then covered and cooked in a little boiling water, and, in my basic recipe, eaten directly from the moulds.

SERVES 4

$2^1/_2$ teaspoons unsalted butter
$^1/_8$ teaspoon salt
$^1/_8$ teaspoon freshly ground black pepper
4 large fresh eggs, preferably from free-range organic chickens
4 slices white bread

1 Butter the inside of four $^1/_2$-cup soufflé moulds with $^1/_2$ teaspoon of the butter and sprinkle each lightly with the salt and pepper, dividing it evenly among the moulds. Break one egg into each mould. In a large saucepan or high-sided frying pan, bring 1 cm ($^1/_2$ in) of water to the boil. Place the moulds in the water and cover the pan with a lid. Boil gently for about 4 minutes, until the whites are set and the yolks still soft inside.

2 Meanwhile, toast the bread and spread one side of each slice with the remaining butter. Trim off the crusts, cut each slice into four thin rectangular strips, and serve with the moulded eggs.

For variations
1 Place 1 tablespoon of cooked peas in the bottom of a buttered mould and break the egg on top. Proceed as indicated above.

2 Sprinkle 1 tablespoon of chopped cooked ham around the yolk of a cooked egg and serve.

THREE VARIATIONS
There are three oeuf cocotte variations here: one with peas, one with ham, and one with herbs which are sprinkled on the bottom and sides of the greased moulds before the eggs are added. This final variation is unmoulded and served on a croûton. These eggs are an excellent vehicle for leftover meat or fish, which can be used as a garnish in the bottom of the moulds. Sauce from a roast or fish dish also makes a nice addition here.

3 Press 2 teaspoons of chopped green herbs (tarragon, chives or chervil, for example) in the bottom and around the sides of a buttered mould. Break an egg into the mould and proceed as indicated above. To serve, run the blade of a sharp knife around the cooked egg and unmould it on a round croûton.

Mushroom Omelette

OMELETTE-MAKING is a special technique that requires some practice, but the result is well worth the effort. This classic version, made with three large fresh eggs, is garnished with thin slices of sautéed mushroom.

MAKES 1 OMELETTE

1 large mushroom
2 teaspoons corn oil
3 large eggs, preferably from a free-range organic chicken
pinch of salt
pinch of freshly ground black pepper
1 teaspoon unsalted butter

1 Cut the cap of the mushroom into slices and the stem into a dice. Heat the oil in a small frying pan. When it is hot, add the sliced and diced mushroom pieces and sauté them in the oil for 45 seconds. Set aside. When cool enough to handle, arrange the mushroom slices in a row on the blade of a knife so they can be slid onto the top of the finished omelette for decoration.

2 In a bowl, beat the eggs with a fork and season them with the salt and pepper. Add the diced mushroom.

3 Heat the butter in 20 cm (8 in) non-stick frying pan. Add the eggs and cook them over medium to high heat, stirring with one hand and vigorously shaking the pan with the other, until small, moist curds form. Stop stirring and allow the pan to sit on the heat for a few seconds, until a light skin forms on the

A CLASSIC TECHNIQUE

This recipe demonstrates how to make a classic French omelette with soft, creamy curds. The idea here is to shake the pan with one hand while moving the flat base of a fork through the eggs with the other, so that the curds are very small. If the eggs are not mixed quickly enough, the curds harden. As soon as most of the mixture holds together, it is left for a few seconds so that enough of a skin can form on the underside of the omelette that it can be rolled together and inverted onto a plate.

underside of the omelette. Loosen the omelette around the edges and gently roll it so that both 'lips' or edges join together.

4 Invert the omelette onto a plate and garnish it with the sliced mushrooms. Serve.

Buttermilk Bread

THIS bread is very dense and freezes well, although it will keep a few days without freezing. Cut into very thin slices, it is ideal for breakfast with the *Smoked Salmon Mould* (page 46), but also goes well with caviar, smoked salmon or the like.

SERVES 3-10

1 envelope active dry yeast
1/2 cup tepid water from the tap, about 110°F (45°C)
1 tablespoon sugar
50 g (2 oz) unsalted butter
2 cups whole wheat flour, about 275 g (10 oz)
1 cup buttermilk, plus additional for brushing on the loaf before baking
1 teaspoon salt
1/2 teaspoon corn oil

1 Place the yeast, water and sugar in the bowl of a food processor and allow to proof for 10 minutes. Add the butter, wholewheat flour, bread flour buttermilk and salt, and process for 1 minute. Oil a large bowl, and place the dough in the bowl. Set aside to proove, covered, for 2 hours.

2 Punch the dough down into the bowl and shape it into a ball about 15 cm (6 in) in diameter. Place the ball of dough on a baking sheet and cover with the overturned bowl. Allow to proove for 1 hour more.

3 Pre-heat the oven to gas mark 6, 400°F (200°C). Brush the dough with the additional buttermilk. Using a sharp knife, make a criss-cross slash on the top of the round loaf. Place in the pre-heated oven for 45 to 50 minutes, until hollow sounding when tapped. Cool to room temperature, slice and serve.

Rolls and Baguettes

MADE in a food processor, these rolls and baguettes are quick to make, thick, and crusty. Smart cooks know that the secret of any good-tasting sandwich is the bread. This easy–to–bake recipe for an all-purpose bread dough is used in preparing any number of sandwiches. When baked as a baguette, it can be thinly sliced, spread with a delicious tomato mixture and then quickly grilled, as in *Olive and Tomato Toasts* (page 114). Or, when shaped and then baked as a large loaf, it can be hallowed out and filled with meat and vegetables, as in *Pan Bagna* (page 115).

MAKES 2 BAGUETTES AND 6 ROLLS

2 envelopes active dry yeast
2 cups tepid water about 110°F (45°C)
1/2 teaspoon sugar
4 1/2 cups bread flour, 600g (1lb 5 oz)
1 cup rolled wheat, 75 g (3 oz)
1 1/2 teaspoons salt
1–2 teaspoons groundnut oil
1 teaspoon yellow cornmeal
1 teaspoon plain flour

1 Place the yeast, water and sugar in the bowl of a food processor and let proove for 5 minutes. Add the bread flour, rolled wheat and salt to the processor bowl and process for 1-2 minutes, until the ingredients form a ball. Grease a

A WORD ABOUT DOUGH

Depending on the temperature and humidity at the time of the year when you bake the bread, the quantity of yeast may need adjusting. If the weather is particularly humid, for example, 1 1/2 envelopes of yeast may be sufficient for 4 1/2 cups of flour. Be sure to dip your measuring cup directly into the flour and then level it off to get the proper amount of flour, which is 600 g (1 lb 5 oz) for 4 1/2 cups.

BROWN AND SERVE TECHNIQUE

At home, I often partially bake rolls and baguettes, removing them from the oven after 12 to 15 minutes, when they have achieved maximum size, but are not yet brown. Let the loaves cool until lukewarm, wrap tightly, and freeze. When needed, unwrap the frozen bread and place it directly on the centre rack of an oven preheated to gas mark 6, 400°F (200°C). Bake for 15 minutes, until brown and crusty.

bowl with half the groundnut oil and place the dough in the bowl. Cover with plastic wrap, and let proove at room temperature for $1^1/_2$ –2 hours, until double or triple in bulk.

2 Push down gently on the dough to let the air out. Place it on a large baking sheet and, using your hands, spread it out to a rectangle about 36×23cm (14×9in), oiling your hands lightly if the dough sticks. Cut the rectangle into four strips, then move two strips to one side of the sheet, and sprinkle them on both sides with half the cornmeal. They should be extended the length of the sheet into two baguettes.

3 Cut each of the two remaining strips into three rectangles. Arrange these next to the uncut strips and sprinkle them on both sides with the remaining cornmeal.

4 Oil the loaves and rolls lightly on top with the remaining groundnut oil and cover them gently with a sheet of plastic wrap. The oil will prevent the plastic wrap from sticking to the loaves when it is removed after proofing. The plastic wrap prevents the dough from drying out and crusting on top.

5 Let the loaves and rolls proove for 45 minutes–1 hour, until double in bulk. Sprinkle the tops with the teaspoon of plain flour. Make a lengthwise slash or criss-cross slashes down the centre of each loaf and roll with a sharp knife.

6 Pre-heat the oven to gas mark 8, 450°F (230°C). Place the bread in the preheated oven and immediately throw 2 tablespoons of water onto the oven floor and close the oven door quickly. This produces steam, which helps create bread with a crustier exterior. Repeat this procedure 5 minutes later.

7 Bake the loaves and rolls for a total of 22–25 minutes (checking them after 15 minutes and placing another tray under them if they are browning too quickly). Remove from the oven when they are dark brown and sound hollow when tapped with a spoon or knife. Cool on a rack.

Croque-Monsieur

THE *croque-monsieur* is a classic toasted ham and cheese sandwich. I make it here with Gruyère cheese, as is traditional in France. Cut into little squares as it emerges from the oven, it makes a terrific hot hors d'oeuvre. You can vary it – for a *croque-madame,* for example, replace the ham with a slice of chicken.

SERVES 4

2 tablespoon corn oil
8 slices white bread, 175 g (6 oz)
8 slices Gruyère cheese, about 100 g (4 oz)
4 slices honey-cured ham, 100 g (4 oz)

1 Pre-heat the oven to gas mark 6, 400°F (200°C).

2 Grease a baking sheet with the oil. Dip the bread slices (on one side only) in the oil, and arrange them, oiled side up, on the table.

3 Place a slice of cheese on top of each slice of bread. Arrange a slice of ham on four of the cheese-covered bread slices, invert the remaining cheese-covered bread slices on top and press together.

4 Dip both sides of the sandwiches in the remaining oil on the tray, and place the tray in the pre-heated oven for 10 minutes.

5 To serve, trim the crusts from the bread and cut the sandwiches diagonally into triangles. Serve hot.

James Beard's Onion Sandwiches

I FIRST tasted this great combination when I went to see James Beard one Sunday morning in the mid 1960s. Ever since, these onion sandwiches have been a favourite at my house. Rolled on its edge in mayonnaise and then in chopped chives, the sandwich is as attractive as it is delicious.

SERVES 4

8 thin slices white bread, 225 g (8 oz)
6 tablespoons mayonnaise
4 teaspoons Dijon mustard
4 slices red onion, cut 2.5 mm (1/8 in) thick from an onion about 9 cm (3 1/2 in) in diameter
4 tablespoons finely chopped chives

1 Arrange the bread slices next to one another on a flat work surface and, using a glass or a round cutter, cut circles as large as possible out of the slices.

2 Spread each bread circle with 1 teaspoon of the mayonnaise and then with 1/2 teaspoon of the mustard. Place an onion slice on four of the bread discs (it should cover to the edge). Top with the remaining bread circles. Press lightly to make them adhere.

3 Spread remaining mayonnaise on the outside edge of each sandwich (about 2 teaspoons per sandwich), and then roll the edge in the chives until coated. Press lightly to make them adhere. Serve.

Smoked Salmon and Cucumber Sandwiches

MADE with smoked salmon and a delicious cucumber relish, this sandwich can be assembled in just a few minutes.

SERVES 4

Cucumber Relish

$^{2}/_{3}$ cup of hot water

$^{1}/_{3}$ cup white distilled vinegar

$^{1}/_{2}$ teaspoon salt

$^{1}/_{2}$ teaspoon sugar

1 cucumber 350 g (12 oz), peeled, seeded and sliced crosswise very thinly

1 shallot, peeled and sliced very thin

$1^{1}/_{2}$ teaspoons finely minced Jalapeño or chilli pepper

2 tablespoons chopped coriander leaves

8 slices white bread

6 slices smoked salmon, about 225 g (8 oz) total

1 In a bowl combine the hot water, vinegar, salt and sugar. Stir in the cucumber, shallot, Jalapeño pepper and coriander. Allow the mixture to marinate for at least one hour before using, or cover and keep for up to 2 weeks in the refrigerator.

2 At serving time, toast the bread. Drain the cucumbers and arrange half of them on 4 slices of toasted bread. Place the salmon slices on top of the cucumbers; top with remaining cucumbers.

3 Arrange the remaining pieces of toast on top and trim off the crusts. Cut each sandwich in half to create 2 rectangles and serve immediately.

CUCUMBER RELISH

This simple, fresh-tasting relish has become a standard ingredient at my house. It keeps for weeks in the refrigerator and is delicious on any sandwich and as an accompaniment to grilled meat or fish. The use of the relish here eliminates the need for butter or mayonnaise, making for a lighter, more savoury sandwich.

Roasted Aubergine Sandwiches

AUBERGINE sandwiches are different and delicious. They feature thin slices of sautéed aubergine layered with dried tomatoes, fresh basil and mozzarella cheese on a home-made French roll.

MAKES 4 SANDWICHES

1 cup sun-dried (not reconstituted) tomatoes, (about 40 g (1½ oz)

1 tablespoon virgin olive oil

¼ cup corn oil

1 aubergine, about 450g (1 lb), cut into 16 slices, each about 1cm (½ in) thick.

Salt and freshly ground pepper to taste

4 oval rolls (see Rolls and Baguettes, page 108)

100 g (4 oz) mozzarella cheese, sliced thin or grated

12 large basil leaves

1 In a saucepan, bring 1½ cups of water to the boil. Add the sun-dried tomatoes and soak for about 10 minutes. Drain (reserving the liquid for stock) and mix the tomatoes with the olive oil.

2 Heat 1 tablespoon of the corn oil in each of two non-stick frying pans and when hot, place 4 slices of aubergine in each pan. Sprinkle with salt and pepper and cook 5 minutes on each side over a medium heat. Remove to a dish and repeat with the remaining oil and aubergine.

3 Pre-heat the oven to gas mark 6, 400°F (200°C). Split the rolls in half and place them, cut side up, on the table. Place 2 slices of aubergine on the bottom half of each roll. Divide the reconstituted tomato halves on top of the aubergine and arrange 3 basil leaves on top. Cover with 3 thin slices (or grated equivalent) of cheese. Sprinkle, if desired, with a little salt and pepper, and add the remaining aubergine slices, 2 per roll. Put the top half of the rolls in place and arrange the assembled sandwiches on a tray.

DRIED TOMATOES

This recipe makes use of dried tomatoes that you reconstitute yourself quite inexpensively (as opposed to buying the costly commercial reconstituted tomatoes in oil). After soaking the tomatoes in boiling water, transfer them to a jar and mix in a little olive oil. To create a concoction of your own, add whatever garnishes you like – from sliced garlic to sprigs of rosemary, walnuts or hazelnut pieces, or hot peppers. Use this mixture on pasta as well as on sandwiches.

4 Bake in the pre-heated oven for 10–12 minutes, until the cheese inside is completely melted. Cut into halves and serve.

Olive and Tomato Toasts

THESE 'toasts' – either baked and served hot from the oven or unbaked and served at room temperature – are great to pass around at large parties. The fresh tomatoes, cut into little cubes, have a sweet taste that goes so well with the concentrated taste of the oil-cured black olives.

SERVES 4

4 tablespoons virgin olive oil
16 slices from a baguette, cut 1 cm ($^1/_2$ in) thick
2 tomatoes, seeded and cut into 5 mm ($^1/_4$ in) dice
$^1/_2$ cup oil-cured black olives, pitted and cut into 5mm ($^1/_4$ in) pieces
4 tablespoons fresh coriander chopped
$^1/_2$ teaspoon freshly ground black pepper
$^1/_4$ teaspoon salt
$1^1/_2$ tablespoons grated Parmesan cheese

1 Pre-heat the oven to gas Mark 6, 400°F (200°C). Spread 2 tablespoons of the olive oil on a baking sheet and dip both sides of the bread slices in the oil. Arrange on the sheet and bake in the pre-heated oven for 6–8 minutes, until lightly browned. Remove from oven and set aside.

2 Meanwhile, in a bowl combine the tomatoes, olives, remaining 2 tablespoons olive oil, coriander, pepper and salt.

3 Divide and spread the mixture evenly on top of each piece of toast. Sprinkle with grated cheese.

4 Return to the oven for 5 minutes and serve warm, or serve unbaked at room temperature.

Pan Bagna

THIS light, healthy picnic sandwich is especially good when made ahead – preferably the day before – on a large round bread loaf.

SERVES 4

1/2 cucumber, about 200 g (7 oz)

1 round crusty country-style loaf of bread, about 450 g (1 lb)

18 black oil-cured olives, pitted and chopped

3 cloves garlic, peeled, crushed, and finely chopped

10 small anchovy fillets, coarsely chopped, 50 g (2 oz) can

2 tablespoons virgin olive oil

4–5 thin slices of red onion

1/3 green pepper, 50 g (2 oz), seeded and sliced thinly

1 ripe tomato, sliced thinly

1/4 teaspoon salt

1/4 teaspoon freshly ground black pepper

12 large basil leaves

1 Peel the cucumber and slice it lengthwise with a vegetable peeler into long thin strips, discarding the seedy centre.

2 Cut the loaf of bread in half horizontally.

3 In a bowl mix together the olives, garlic, anchovies (with their oil) and olive oil. Spread the mixture on the cut surface of both bread halves, then arrange the slices of onion, green pepper and tomatoe on the bottom half of the loaf. Sprinkle with salt and pepper, arrange the basil leaves and then the cucumber slices on top.

BATHED BREAD

Pan Bagna literally means 'bathed bread'. It originally consisted of a salad of different vegetables – from tomatoes to onions, red pepper, and garlic – that were mixed with pieces of leftover bread so that the bread was soaked with vegetable juices. In the more modern version, salad ingredients are placed in a split loaf of bread. The loaf is then wrapped and weighted down. The juices flow through the bread and the filling becomes compact enough so that the loaf can be cut into pieces.

4 Invert the top half of the bread to reform the loaf and wrap it tightly in plastic wrap. Refrigerate for 2–3 hours with a 2.25 kg (5 lb) weight on top (canned goods or a milk carton). This enables the juices in the filling to flow through the bread.

5 At serving time, unwrap the loaf and cut it into wedges to serve.

Jam 'Sandwiches'

JAM sandwiches are fun to make for a party. Consisting of thin slices of firm-textured pound cake spread with different flavoured jams, these can be served stacked up together in traditional 'sandwich' fashion, or they can be served open-face, with a colourful jam spread on the surface of each cake slice. To add diversity to a dessert tray, select the flavours to suit your own tastes, cutting each one into a different shape.

SERVES 4

175 g (6 oz) fine-textured pound cake, madeira cake or similar
1½ tablespoons raspberry jam
1½ tablespoons apricot jam
1½ tablespoons strawberry jam

Note:
The piece of pound cake I used was 15 cm (6 in) long by 13 cm (5 in) wide

1 Trim the outside of the cake and cut it into six slices, each 5 mm (¼ in) thick. Spread the raspberry jam on the top surface of one slice, the apricot jam on the top surface of another slice, and the strawberry jam on the top surface of a third slice.

2 Top with the remaining cake slices to create three 'sandwiches'. Cut each 'sandwich' into different shapes: one into squares, one into triangles, and one into rectangles.

3 Arrange on a plate and serve.

Desserts

Almond Cake with Mango Coulis
Baked Apple Tart
Caramelized Apple Timbales
Baked Apricots with Almonds
Baked Bananas in Lemon-Rum Sauce
Blueberries with Brown Sugar
Cherry Bread Pudding
Chocolate and Fruit Nut Cups
Chocolate Mint Truffles
Chocolate Soufflé Cake with Raspberry-Rum Sauce
Coffee Crème Caramel
Orange and Grapefruit Segments
Figs Villamora
Calimyrna Figs in Spicy Port Sauce
Fresh Fruit with Minted Apricot Fondue
Grapes and Raisins in Lime Biscuit Cones
Hazelnut Parfait with Candied Violets
Oranges in Grand Marnier
Crêpes Soufflés in Grapefruit Sauce
Salpicon of Pineapple
Baked Pears with Figs
Pistachio Floating Island with Blackcurrant Sauce
Raspberry Granité
Strawberry Buttermilk Shortcakes
Candied Orange Rind

Almond Cake with Mango Coulis

COLOURFUL mango *coulis*, flavoured with rum and a bit of honey, is the perfect accompaniment to my favourite almond cake. Be sure to only use very ripe mangoes! For a more festive presentation, sprinkle additional flaked almonds on the batter just before baking.

SERVES 10

1 tablespoon plus 1/2 teaspoon corn oil

1 1/2 cups flaked almonds

3/4 cup granulated sugar

1/4 cup potato flour

1 tablespoon unsalted butter, softened

1 teaspoon vanilla extract

3 egg yolks

2 tablespoons milk

5 egg whites

Mango Coulis

1 ripe mango, about 450 g (1 lb)

1/4 cup water

2 tablespoons dark rum

1 tablespoons lemon juice

2 tablespoons honey

CAKE TECHNIQUES

To make this traditional cake less calorific, I have drastically reduced the amount of butter and the number of egg yolks. Be sure that the egg whites are beaten until fairly firm, and that they are folded into the almond batter quickly enough so they don't have a chance to deflate. Folding should take only a few seconds with a spatula. Transfer to the greased baking tin and bake immediately in the oven.

1 Pre-heat oven to gas mark 3, 325°F (160°C). Grease the bottom and sides of a 20 cm (8 in) cake time with 1/2 tsp vegetable oil and line the bottom of the tin with greaseproof paper.

2 In a bowl of a food processor, place the almonds, 1/4 cup of the sugar and the potato flour. Process until the nuts are finely ground. Add the butter, remaining oil, all but two of the sugar, vanilla, egg yolks and milk and process just until the mixture is smooth. Transfer it to a bowl.

3 In another bowl, beat the egg whites until firm, then add the reserved 2 tablespoons of sugar and beat for a few seconds longer.

4 Folk the egg white mixture into the almond mixture and transfer the batter to the greased tin. Bake in the pre-heated oven for 35 minutes, or until set. Cool on a rack.

For mango coulis:

1 Cut the mango in half lengthwise and scoop out the flesh. Place the flesh in the bowl of a food processor and process until smooth. Add the water, rum, lemon juice and honey and process until smooth.

2 To serve, remove the cake from the tin, cut it into wedges, and serve it with the mango coulis.

Baked Apple Tart

CORED, halved apples filled with apricot jam are wrapped in a round of pastry dough and dusted with a sprinkling of sugar before baking. I prefer serving this tart at room temperature.

SERVES 4

Dough

3/4 cup plain flour, 75 g (3 oz)
3 tablespoon unsalted butter, cold
1/2 teaspoon granulated sugar
2 tablespoons water, ice cold

Filling

2 large Golden Delicious apples, 450 g (1 lb)
2 tablespoons apricot jam
1 tablespoon granulated sugar
1/2 tablespoon unsalted butter

CLASSIC DOUGH

The classic dough for this dessert is suitable for most baking needs and is easily made in a food processor. It is important that you not overmix the ingredients, however. The butter should not be totally incorporated into the flour; visible pieces will melt as the dough cooks and it will develop some of the flakiness evident in puff pastry. Notice that there is no waste; the dough is rolled free-form on a cookie sheet and the edges folded back over the apples, so trimming is not required, as it would be if the tart were made in a conventional pie plate.

For dough:

1 Pre-heat the oven to gas mark 6, 400°F (200°C).

2 In the bowl of a food processor, place the flour, butter (cut into 1 cm 1/2 in pieces) and sugar. Process for 5 seconds, and then add the water and process for another 5 seconds. Remove the dough, even if not compactly mixed, and press it between two layers of plastic wrap. Roll it out to form a circle about 25 cm (10 in) in diameter. Transfer to a baking sheet and refrigerator.

For filling:

1 Meanwhile, peel the apples and cut them in half. Remove the cores and hollow them out a little with a measuring spoon. Chop the trimmings obtained from hollowing out the fruit (you should have about 3/4 cup). Place 1/2 table-spoon jam in the hollow of each apple half and arrange the halves, cut side down, in the centre of the circle of dough. Sprinkle the chopped apple around the halves.

2 Bring the edge of the dough up over the apples to create a border, 2.5–5 cm (1–2 in) high, around the edge. (This will create a receptacle that will hold the cooking juices inside.)

3 Sprinkle the top of the tart with sugar and dot with butter. Bake in the pre-heated oven for 45 minutes to 1 hour, until well browned and crusty. Serve warm or at room temperature.

Caramelized Apple Timbales

THIS dessert is easy to make ahead. Arrange the cooked, caramelized apples in tiny, plastic-lined soufflé moulds so they are easy to unmould. Notice that the apples are not peeled; the skin gives some chewiness and texture to the dish. The concentrated taste is particularly pleasing when the timbales are served with a little sour cream or plain yoghurt.

SERVES 4

4 large Golden Delicious apples about 750 g ($1^1/_2$ lb)
2 teaspoons julienned lemon rind
4 tablespoons granulated sugar
3 tablespoons water plus $^1/_3$ cup water
2 tablespoons lemon juice
1 tablespoon unsalted butter
4 tablespoons sour cream or plain yoghurt

1 Remove the apple stems with a little adjoining skin and flesh and place them in a bowl with lemon juice. Set aside for use as a decoration.

2 Cut the apples in half lengthwise and core them. Then cut each half crosswise into 5 mm ($^1/_4$ in) thick slices to make about 6 loosely packed cups.

3 In a frying pan, combine the sugar and 3 tablespoons water and cook over a medium high heat until the mixture turns into a dark brown caramel (about 3–4 minutes). Add the apple slices, the lemon rind, $^1/_3$ cup water and butter. Mix well, reduce the heat, and cook at a gentle boil, covered, for about 7 minutes. (The apples should be tender and most of the moisture gone.) Remove the lid and cook, rolling the apples in the caramel, for about 5 minutes over high heat until the juice has turned again into caramel and the apple pieces are browned. Let cool to lukewarm.

4 Meanwhile, line four small soufflé moulds or ramekins (about $^1/_2$ to $^3/_4$ cup capacity) with plastic wrap. Pack the lukewarm apple mixture into the moulds, cover with plastic wrap and refrigerate until cold.

5 At serving time, unmould the timbales and decorate them with the reserved apple stems. Serve with a tablespoon of sour cream or yoghurt.

Baked Apricots with Almonds

THE success of this dish depends on the quality of the apricots you use. If you have very ripe, full-flavoured fruit, preferably from an organic farm, you will have terrific results. I used to make this dessert with a lot of double cream; now I use just a little milk. If you want to go one step further, eliminate the milk and add a few tablespoons of water to lend a little moisture to the fruit.

SERVES 6

450 g (1 lb) ripe apricots (about 6 or 7)
3 tablespoons apricot jam
1/4 cup milk
2 tablespoons sliced almonds
1 tablespoon granulated sugar

1 Pre-heat the oven to gas mark 4, 350°F (180°C).

2 Cut the apricots in half and remove their pits.

3 Arrange the apricot halves, cut side down, in a gratin dish. Spoon the jam over the fruit, and pour the milk around the fruit. Sprinkle the almonds and sugar on top.

4 Place in the pre-heated oven for 30–35 minutes. Serve lukewarm or at room temperature.

Baked Bananas in Lemon and Rum Sauce

BANANAS are almost nature's perfect food – high in potassium, calcium, and Vitamins A, B, and C. Available year round, they are best when little black spots begin to form on the skin, indicating they are very ripe. You will notice that the skin blackens completely after 15 minutes of cooking. At that point, you can remove the fruit and simply serve it with a little lemon juice or with the tart-lemon-rum sauce below.

SERVES 4

4 very ripe bananas, with black-spotted skin, about 1 kg (2 lb)

Lemon and Rum Sauce
1 tablespoon grated lemon rind
2 tablespoons lemon juice
2 tablespoons granulated sugar
3 tablespoons orange marmalade
1/4 cup water
2 tablespoons dark rum
Mint leaves, for garnish
Strips of orange peel, for garnish

1 Pre-heat the oven to gas mark 6, 400°F (200°C).

2 Trim the ends of the bananas, removing about 1 cm (1/2 in) from each end, and cut a slit through the skin extending the length of the fruit. Arrange the unpeeled bananas on a baking sheet and place in the pre-heated oven for 15 minutes. (The skin will turn black.)

3 Meanwhile, in a saucepan mix together the lemon rind, lemon juice, sugar, marmalade and water and bring the mixture to a boil. Boil for 1 minute, then transfer to a serving dish.

4 As soon as the bananas are cool enough to handle, remove the skin and place them in the sauce. Using a spoon, coat the bananas on all sides with the sauce.

5 When cool, stir in the rum and decorate the bananas with mint leaves and orange peel. Serve.

Blueberries with Brown Sugar

THIS is a simple, delicious summer recipe. Look over the blueberries carefully and remove and discard any damaged ones. If you wash them, dry them off with kitchen paper so the water doesn't dilute the yoghurt. The best way to serve the berries is to arrange them on individual plates, create a well in the centre, and then spoon the yoghurt into the well and sprinkle it with the brown sugar. If you desire a richer dessert, substitute sour cream or whipped cream for the yoghurt, and sprinkle it with brown sugar.

SERVES 4

550 g (1 1/4 lb) blueberries
8 tablespoons plain yoghurt
4 tablespoons dark brown sugar
Mint leaves, for garnish

1 Divide the blueberries among four plates. Make a well in the centre of the berries and spoon in some yoghurt.

2 Sprinkle the berries and yoghurt with the brown sugar, decorate with a few mint leaves, and serve.

Note:
The sugar will melt and spread somewhat on the yoghurt, giving the dessert an interesting look.

Cherry Bread Pudding

THIS is a great dessert to make when cherries are in full season. You can make the same recipe with berries or pieces of plum instead of cherries. Flavour them with the almond-sugar mixture, too. This dessert is best served lukewarm with a little sour cream or, if you prefer, yoghurt.

SERVES 6

450 g (1 lb) ripe cherries, 400 g (14 oz) pitted
3 slices white bread, toasted
1 cup milk
1/2 cup sliced almonds, toasted
1/2 cup cherry preserve
1 teaspoon unsalted butter
4 teaspoons granulated sugar
1/2 teaspoon confectioners' sugar
1 cup sour cream or yoghurt

1 Pre-heat the oven to gas mark 4, 350°F (180°C).

2 Pit the cherries. Then coarsely crumble the toasted bread (you should have 1 cup) and place it in a bowl with the milk. Mix well, and add the cherries, toasted almonds (reserving 2 tbsp) and the cherry preserve.

3 In another bowl, mix the reserved almonds with 2 teaspoons of the sugar.

4 Grease a 1.5 litre (2 1/2 pint) gratin dish with the butter and sprinkle it with the remaining 2 teaspoons of sugar. Pour the cherry mixture into the dish and top with the almond-sugar mixture.

5 Bake in the pre-heated oven for 35–40 minutes. Cool to lukewarm, sprinkle with confectioners' sugar and serve with sour cream or yoghurt, if desired.

Chocolate and Fruit Nut Cups

THESE 'cups' are more a candy or *petit four* than a dessert. They are especially fun to make with children, who love to select their own assortment of fruits and nuts and press them into the soft chocolate. The result is beautiful and delicious and if you can refrain from eating more than two of them, the calorie intake is not too frightening.

SERVES 6

100g (4oz) bittersweet chocolate
1 tablespoon sliced almonds
1 tablespoon pecan pieces
1 tablespoon pumpkin seeds
1 tablespoon golden raisins
1 tablespoon raisins
1 large strawberry, cut into 12 wedges
3 mint leaves, cut in pieces
12 small foil or paper cups 4 cm (1 1/2 in) diameter by 2.5cm (1 in) deep

1 Melt the chocolate in a double boiler or in a microwave oven. (You should have about 1/3 cup of melted chocolate.) Divide the melted chocolate among the 12 cups, filling the base of each with about 5 mm (1/4 in) of chocolate.

2 While the chocolate is still liquid, arrange the nuts, pumpkin seeds, raisins, strawberry wedges and mint leaves on top and press on them lightly to partially imbed them in the chocolate. Refrigerate for about 1 hour, until hardened.

3 To serve, remove the 'cups' from their foil or paper casing, arrange them on a plate and serve.

Chocolate Mint Truffles

THERE are about 30 calories in each of these small truffles, not as many as you might expect, considering their rich flavour. These are especially nice to box and give to friends over the holiday season. They keep well in the refrigerator and can also be frozen.

MAKES 20 SMALL TRUFFLES

100 g (4 oz) bittersweet chocolate
2 tablespoons milk
1 egg yolk
2 teaspoons finely chopped mint
2 teaspoons unsweetened cocoa powder

1 Place the chocolate and milk together, either in a double boiler over hot water, or in a microwave oven set at medium level for 30 seconds at a time. Heat until the chocolate has melted.

2 Stir to combine, then add the egg yolk and mint, and mix well. (At this point, the mixture can be heated in a double boiler to 140°F (60°C) and held at that temperature for 3–4 minutes to kill any possible salmonella bacteria in the egg yolk.)

3 Cool the mixture to room temperature and then cover and refrigerate it for at least 1 hour until firm.

4 Divide the cold chocolate mixture into 20 small pieces and press each piece into a roundish ball. (The balls should be uneven so they look more like real truffles.) Sprinkle cocoa over the balls on the plate, shaking the plate so the truffles roll around in the cocoa and become coated.

5 Transfer the truffles to a clean plate and refrigerate them until serving time.

Chocolate Soufflé Cake with Raspberry-Rum Sauce

THIS light cake containing fewer egg yolks and less starch and butter than is customary for this type of dessert, is fluffy and delicate. Serve at room temperature, with or without the sauce.

SERVES 6-8

2 tablespoons plus 1 teaspoon canola oil

175 g (6 oz) dark bittersweet chocolate

1/4 cup unsalted butter

1/4 cup granulated sugar

2 tablespoons arrowroot

2 egg yolks

6 egg whites

1/2 teaspoon confectioners' sugar

Raspberry-Rum Sauce

1/2 cup raspberry preserve (preferably seedless)

1 tablespoon dark rum

1 Pre-heat the oven to gas mark 3, 325°F (160°C).

2 Grease a round cake tin measuring 23 cm (9 in) across and 7.5 cm (3 in) deep with 1 teaspoon oil.

3 Combine the chocolate, butter, 2 tablespoons remaining oil and sugar in the top of a double boiler (or in a microwave-safe bowl). Cook over boiling water (or in a microwave) until the chocolate and butter have melted. Stir to combine. Add the arrowroot and mix it in with a whisk. Then whisk in the egg yolks; the mixture will thicken.

4 Whip egg whites until firm and fold them lightly and quickly into the chocolate mixture. Pour the batter into the tin and place it in the pre-heated oven for about 30 minutes. The cake should still be a little soft in the centre.

5 Let cool to lukewarm. Invert onto a plate, and then invert back onto a serving platter. Sprinkle with confectioners' sugar.

For sauce:

1 In a bowl, combine the raspberry preserve (straining it first if using preserves with seeds) with the rum and 1 tablespoon of water.

2 Arrange a slice of cake on each dessert dish with some sauce alongside.

Coffee Crème Caramel

YOU can make the caramel for this light dessert in a separate pan, but it simplifies the preparation if you make it right in the casserole dish where you make the dessert. Keep a pan of cold water handy, however, and dip the base of the casserole in the water if the caramel continues to cook and darken after it is removed from the heat. If you prepare the caramel in a separate pan, add additional sugar to accommodate the amount of caramel lost when you transfer it to the casserole.

SERVES 4

Caramel
2 tablespoons sugar
1 tablespoon water

$1^{1}/_{2}$ cups milk
2 tablespoons granulated sugar
1 tablespoon instant expresso coffee
1 egg
1 egg white

1 Pre-heat the oven to gas mark 4, 350°F (180°C).

2 In a 2-cup ceramic or metal casserole that can be used over direct heat, combine the sugar and water and cook over medium heat until caramelized, about 4–5 minutes. Set aside.

3 In a saucepan, combine the milk, sugar and coffee. Warm the mixture just enough to melt the instant coffee. Whisk in the whole egg and egg white. Pour mixture through a strainer over the caramel.

4 Set the casserole dish in a larger pan and surround it with warm tap water. Place in the pre-heated oven and bake for 50–60 minutes, until set, checking from time to time to make sure the water does not boil. (If it does, add a few ice cubes to cool it to below the boil.)

5 Cool for at least 4 hours and then unmould to serve.

Orange and Grapefruit Segments

THIS is an attractive dish, especially if you use blood oranges, which contrast nicely with the grapefruit. In addition to using the flesh of the oranges and grapefruits, I mix the juice squeezed from the membranes of both fruits with a little honey to create a sauce. Garnished with mint and julienned orange skin, this makes a delightful dinner dessert with a slice of sponge cake or biscuits.

SERVES 4

2 seedless navel or blood oranges, 225–275 g (8-10 oz) each

2 ruby red grapefruits, 450 g (1 lb) each

2 tablespoons honey

2 tablespoons, julienned orange skin, for garnish

Mint leaves, for garnish

1 With a vegetable peeler, remove about 6 strips of peel from one of the oranges and cut the strips into a fine julienne. Cut the peel (including the white pith underneath) from the oranges and the grapefruits.

2 With a sharp knife, remove the orange and grapefruit segments from between the membranes, and then squeeze the membranes into a bowl to release the juices. (You should have 1 cup of combined juices.) Whisk the honey into the juice until combined.

3 Arrange alternating segments of orange and grapefruit in four dishes and pour the sweetened juice over them. Garnish with mint leaves and julienned orange peel. Serve cold.

Figs Villamora

THIS is a great snack food, very high in fibre and terrific with a glass of sweet port wine from Portugal, some Gorgonzola cheese and a loaf of crusty bread. This recipe uses Black Mission figs from America.

SERVES 4-6

450 g (1 lb) dried figs (dark), about 24

48 whole shelled, unpeeled almonds

1 Split the figs in half starting at the base, but leave them attached at the stem end. Split each half in half again in the same way, and gently press the figs, skin-side-up, on the table. (They should look like flowers or four-leaf clovers with each 'petal' or 'leaf' still attached at the stem.)

2 When all the figs have been split and pressed, make a sandwich with 2 figs, pressing them together, flesh against flesh. Then, push the almonds, rounded ends first, about a third of the way into the figs where the 'petals' connect near the stem, and press to ensure that the almonds are held securely.

3 Heat the oven to gas mark 4, 350°F (180°C). Spread the fig 'flowers' on a tray, and place the tray in the oven for 20 minutes to brown the almonds and dry the figs (which concentrates their flavour).

4 Let cool and then store in a container, tightly covered, until ready to serve. They will keep for up to 2 weeks.

FROM VILLAMORA, PORTUGAL

Villamora is a town in the southern part of Portugal where you can find dried figs prepared like this in the market. To facilitate the shaping of these, try to get the largest dried figs that you can find. The figs are partially split, spread out, and 'sandwiched' together with almonds inserted in the corners. These are then dried in the oven to concentrate the taste of the figs and brown the almonds.

Figs in Spicy Port Sauce

THIS is a nice combination because you have the sweetness and intense flavour of dried figs complemented by port wine. However, the sweetness of the wine is lessened somewhat by the bitter Campari, whose flavour is enhanced by cayenne pepper.

SERVES 6

450 g (1 lb) dried figs (Calimyma, if available) about 20
$1^1/_2$ cups water
1 cup port wine
$^1/_4$ cup Campari
Pinch of cayenne pepper
1 teaspoon cornflour dissolved in 1 tablespoon water
1 cup plain yoghurt

1 Stand the figs in a large saucepan and add the water. Cover, bring to the boil over a high heat, and boil gently for 5 minutes. Add the port, Campari and cayenne pepper, bring back to the boil, cover, and boil for another 5 minutes.

2 Stir in the dissolved cornflour, mix well and return to the boil. Remove from the heat and cool the figs in the cooking liquid.

3 To serve, divide the yoghurt and spread it on to six serving plates. Arrange the figs on top of the yoghurt, 3 or 4 to each plate, and spoon some cooking liquid over them. Serve.

CALIMYRNA FIGS

The name 'Calimyrna' is an acronym used to describe a variety of figs grown in California but native to Smyrna, Turkey. When dried, these are pale yellow or beige and have a thicker wall than Mission figs, which are jet black. I poach them here in water, port wine and Campari, that delightfully bitter-tasting aperitif from Italy. When the mixture has cooled and the liquid around the fruit thickened a little, the figs are served with this natural sauce and yoghurt, lower in calories than sour cream.

Grapes and Raisins in Lime Biscuit Cones

HERE is an impressive, make-ahead dessert worthy of any occasion. A crispy, lime-flavoured biscuit, rolled up into a cone, is filled with a simple mixture of grapes, dried currants and orange juice.

SERVES 6

Cones
1 tablespoon unsalted butter, melted
1 tablespoon corn oil
1 egg white
1/2 teaspoon vanilla extract
1 teaspoon grated lime rind
3 tablespoons plain flour
3 tablespoons sugar
Confectioners' sugar, for decoration

Filling
275g (10 oz) seedless red grapes
1/4 cup dried currants
2 tablespoons orange juice

1 Pre-heat the oven to gas mark 5, 375°F (190°C).

2 Whisk together the melted butter, oil, egg white, vanilla, lime rind, flour and sugar until smooth.

3 Spoon 1 tablespoon of batter at four equally-spaced intervals on a non-stick baking sheet or parchment-lined aluminium baking sheet. Using the back of a spoon in a circular motion, spread each mound of batter until it is very thin and has been extended to a diameter of at least 13cm (5in). Bake until necely browned (some areas will be browner than others), for about 7-8 minutes.

4 Using a large spatula, immediately lift off the biscuits and wrap them, one after another, around a cone-shaped metal mould (mine is 10cm/4in long and

MAKING BISCUIT CONES

For this recipe to work well, it is important to use a heavy, non-stick biscuit sheet. Using the underside of a spoon, spread the batter out on a sheet until it is very, very thin; you should almost be able to see through it. As the biscuits emerge from the oven, wrap them immediately around a cone-shaped mould (or coated paper drinking cup) until they firm. If allowed to cool, rewarm them briefly in the oven to soften before attempting to wrap them around the mould, otherwise they will crack.

has a opening diameter of about 10cm.4in). Remove each biscuit as it firms around the mould and cool the cones on a rack.

For filling:

1 Cut the grapes in half and place them in a bowl. Add the currants and orange juice. Set aside.

2 To serve, dip the open end of the cone in confectioners' sugar, if desired, and arrange on each plate. Spoon about $^{1}/_{2}$ cup of fruit on each plate, so that it appears to be emerging from the cone.

Fresh Fruit with Minted Apricot Fondue

COLOURFUL and multi-textured, this fruit fondue makes an excellent party dessert. Each guest dips pieces of fresh and dried fruit in a sauce made of apricot preserve, minced mint leaves and kirsch. You can also flavour the sauce with rum, cognac, or even whisky, if you prefer, or eliminate the alcohol altogether.

SERVES 4

Apricot Dipping Sauce

1 cup apricot preserve

2 tablespoons kirsch

1 tablespoon mint leaves, finely chopped

1 tablespoon water

1 ripe anjou or Bartlett pear, about 200 g (7 oz)

225g (8 oz) strawberries (8 large) rinsed, hulled, and halved

2 teaspoons lemon juice

1 large seedless orange, peeled, halved, and each half cut into 5 mm ($^{3}/_{8}$ in) slices

12 dried figs

$^{1}/_{3}$ cup dark Muscat raisins

8–10 mint leaves, for garnish

1 In a small, attractive glass serving bowl, mix together the preserve, kirsch, chopped mint leaves and water. Set aside.

2 Peel the pear and cut it into quarters. Remove and discard the seeds. Place the pear, strawberries and lemon juice in a bowl and toss gently to coat the fruit.

3 At serving time, arrange the bowl of dipping sauce in the centre of a platter and surround it with the fresh and dried fruits. Sprinkle with mint and serve, encouraging guests to dip the fresh fruit in the sauce.

Hazelnut Parfait with Candied Violets

THIS hazelnut parfait, or *parfait aux noisettes*, is an ideal party dish because it can be made well ahead of serving. It keeps frozen for several weeks and advantageously replaces ice cream. Since it serves 6 people, each person gets only about 3 tablespoons of cream, which makes it an acceptable choice for special occasions.

SERVES 6

1/4 teaspoon corn oil
1 cup hazelnuts, about 175 g (6 oz)
1 1/4 cups double cream
2 tablespoons granulated sugar
1/2 teaspoon pure vanilla
3 crystallized violets or other candied or crystallized flowers

1 Pre-heat the oven to gas mark 6, 400°F (200°C).

2 Grease a 3-cup soufflé mould with the oil. Cut two long, narrow strips of greaseproof paper and position them in the mould so they form a cross in the bottom and extend up over the sides. Place a round of greaseproof paper in the bottom of the mould. (The paper strips and round will facilitate unmoulding.)

3 Arrange the nuts on a baking sheet and place in the pre-heated oven until lightly browned, about 8 minutes. Transfer the hot nuts to a clean tea towel and rub them in the towel to remove as much skin as possible. (Don't worry if half the skin remains.) Place the nuts in a food processor and process until chopped, but not too fine.

4 Whip the cream with sugar and vanilla until firm and then fold in the nuts. Transfer the mixture to the greased mould. Bang the mould firmly on the table to tighten the mixture and to eliminate air bubbles. Cover with plastic wrap, pressing on it to flatten the top of the parfait. Place in the freezer for 4–5 hours, or longer.

5 At serving time, unmould the soufflé onto a serving plate by pulling gently on the paper strips to help release it from the mould. Crumble the crystallized or candied flowers on top and cut into wedges to serve.

Oranges in Grand Marnier

MAKE this refreshing dessert far enough ahead so that the oranges can cool completely in the cooking syrup. Notice that I use some of the julienned orange rind in this dish, blanching it first to eliminate bitterness. It intensifies the taste and lends texture to the dessert. The oranges are poached just briefly and flavoured with Grand Marnier.

SERVES 4

4 seedless navel oranges, 175 g (6 oz) each
1/4 cup granulated sugar
2 tablespoons Grand Marnier
Additional julienne orange peel, for garnish
Mint leaves, for garnish

1 With a vegetable peeler, cut 2 long, very thin strips of orange peel, each about 2.5 cm (1 in) wide, from each orange. Cut the strips into a julienne (very thin strips), place the julienne in a saucepan and cover with 2 cups of water. Bring to the boil, drain in a colander, rinse under cool water, and return the julienne to the rinsed saucepan with 1 cup water and 1/4 cup sugar. Cook for 3–4 minutes, until large bubbles form and the mixture becomes a syrup.

2 Meanwhile, peel the oranges, removing the white pith under skin as well. Cut the oranges in half crosswise and add to the syrup. Cover and cook over low heat for 3–4 minutes, checking occasionally and adding 1 or 2 tablespoons of water if there is no liquid visible in the pan.

3 Let the oranges cool in the juice and then add the Grand Marnier. Arrange oranges and some juice into each dessert dish. Garnish with additional orange julienne and mint leaves, if desired, and serve.

Crêpes Soufflés in Grapefruit Sauce

THESE crêpes can be made ahead and served unstuffed on their own, with the grapefruit sauce or with jam. In this recipe, I fill them with a low-calorie soufflé mixture made from a combination of stiffened, slightly sweetened egg whites and grated lime rind. This same mixture could be baked without the crêpes in a large greased souffle mould (1.75–2.25 litres/3–4 pint size) for approximately 30 minutes and then served with the grapefruit sauce alongside.

SERVES 6

Grapefruit Sauce

1 ruby red grapefruit, 450 g (1 lb)
1/4 cup grenadine syrup
1 tablespoon lemon juice

Crêpes

1/2 cup plain flour
1 egg
3/4 cup milk
2 tablespoons vegetable oil
1/8 teaspoon granulated sugar

Extra corn oil for greasing pan

Soufle Mixture

5 egg whites
1/4 cup granulated sugar
1 tablespoon grapefruit rind, from grapefruit above
1 teaspoon unsalted butter
6 mint leaves, coarsely chopped, for garnish

CLASSIC TECHNIQUE

I use a very light crêpe batter which contains only one egg and the crêpes are made in a 20 cm (8 in) frying pan. Perhaps the most important thing to remember when making crêpes is to spread the batter very quickly in the hot pan or it will solidify before it coats the bottom of the pan; then, more batter will be required and the resulting crêpe will be too thick. Use a twisting, tilting, and shaking motion to move the batter quickly over the surface of the pan, coating it lightly.

1 Grate the grapefruit (coloured skin only) to obtain 1 tablespoon of rind. Set aside.

For grapefruit sauce:

1 Peel the remainder of the skin from the grapefruit.. With a sharp knife, remove the flesh segments from the surrounding membranes. Squeeze the membranes to obtain 1/2 cup of juice.

2 Cut the segments into 1 cm (1/2 in) pieces (1/2 cup), and combine in a bowl with grapefruit juice, grenadine and lemon juice.

For crêpes:

1 In a bowl, mix flour, egg and 1/4 cup of the milk with a whisk until very smooth. Add the remainder of the milk, oil, salt and sugar, and mix well.

2 Lightly grease the bottom of a 20 cm (8 in) non-stick frying pan and place over a high heat. When hot, add 3 tablespoons of batter and tilt and shake the pan quickly until the batter covers the entire bottom of the pan.

3 Cook for 45 seconds, turn, and cook for 30 seconds on the other side. Continue making crêpes, stacking them on a plate as they are made.

For soufflé mixture

1 Pre-heat the oven to gas mark 5, 375°F (190°C).

2 Beat the egg whites until firm. Add the 3/4 cup sugar and the reserved grapefruit rind all at once, and beat another 15–30 seconds.

3 Lightly grease six 1 1/2-cup ovenproof glass bowls with the butter. Line each of the bowls with a crêpe and spoon the souffle mixture into the centre. Fold the edges of each crêpe up over the soufflé mixture to enclose.

4 Arrange the bowls on a baking tray and place in the pre-heated oven for 8 minutes.

5 To serve, unmould the soufflés and arrange them browned side down (or up, if desired) on individual plates. Spoon some sauce, around each soufflé, and garnish with mint, if desired.

Salpicon of Pineapple

SALPICON means 'to dice' and this dessert consists of diced ripe pineapple that is seasoned with crème de Cassis, cognac and brown sugar. Pineapple is high in potassium, Vitamin C, and iron, and ripeness is important here. If you are fortunate enough to find a particularly sweet pineapple, cut down on the sugar. The dark raisins add colour, providing a nice contrast to the pineapple.

SERVES 6

1 ripe pineapple, 1.5 kg (3 lb)
1/4 cup crème de Cassis
2 tablespoons cognac
3 tablespoons light brown sugar
1 tablespoon dark raisins

1 Trim the pineapple at both ends and cut it lengthwise into quarters. Cut out the core. Cut each quarter in half and remove the wedges of fruit from the skin. Cut each wedge into eight pieces.

2 In a bowl, combine the pineapple pieces with the crème de Cassis, cognac and brown sugar. Refrigerate until serving time.

3 Spoon into dessert bowls and serve, very cold, garnished with the raisins.

Baked Pears with Figs

REPLACE the figs with raisins, if you prefer, or just bake the pears alone with the citrus juices, butter and apricot preserves. This dessert is particularly good when the pears used are ripe and full of flavour; the best choice would be those grown on an organic farm. Use Black Mission figs if possible. Serve at room temperature.

SERVES 4

2 ripe Anjou pears, about 450 g (1 lb)
16 dried figs 225 g, 8 oz
1 tablespoon orange juice
1 tablespoon lemon juice
3/4 cup water
1 tablespoon unsalted butter
1/2 cup water
1 tablespoon apricot preserve
1/2 cup sour cream (optional)

1 Pre-heat the oven to gas mark 6, 400°F (200°C).

2 Peel, halve and core the pears. Cut the figs crosswise into slices, and arrange them in a gratin dish. Place the pears, flat side down, on top of the figs and sprinkle them with the orange and lemon juices and then pour in the water. Dot with butter, and spoon the preserves on top of the pears.

3 Bake the pears in the pre-heated oven for 45 minutes, checking occasionally to ensure that the mixture stays wet so it doesn't burn; if it gets too dry, add a couple of tablespoons of water.

4 Let cool and serve at room temperature with some sour cream, if desired.

Pistachio Floating Island with Blackcurrant Sauce

THIS elegant dessert must be made ahead so it can be cold and set before being unmoulded. In this recipe, I make it in a loaf tin but it can be made in a round tin, too. Except for the small amount of butter used to grease the baking tin, the dessert contains no fat and amounts to only about 200 calories per serving. The colourful, easy-to-make sauce combines two distinct flavours – strawberries and blackcurrants.

SERVES 6

1/2 teaspoon unsalted butter
5 large egg whites (3/4 cup)
1/2 cup granulated sugar
1/3 cup pistachio nuts, shelled and coarsely chopped
2 large strawberries, hulled and cut into 5mm (1/4 in) dice (1/3 cup)

Sauce
275 g (10 oz) strawberries, hulled
275 g (10 oz) natural blackcurrant preserve (with berries)
2 tablespoons crème de Cassis (blackcurrant liqueur)
2 or 3 strawberries, sliced, for garnish
2 tablespoons chopped pistachio nuts, for garnish

1 Pre-heat the oven to gas mark 4, 350°F (180°C).

2 Grease a 1.5 litre (2 1/2 pint) loaf tin with butter. Beat the egg whites until stiff, and then add the sugar all at once and beat for a few seconds. Fold the pistachios and the diced strawberries into the beaten whites, and transfer the mixture to the loaf tin.

3 Place the pan in a bain-marie and surround it with warm tap water. Bake in the pre-heated oven for 30 minutes, then remove the pan from the bain-marie and allow it to cool on a rack. The dessert will deflate slightly. (The recipe can be prepared to this point up to one day ahead, covered with plastic wrap, and refrigerated.)

For sauce:
1 Slice 2 or 3 strawberries for use as a decoration, and set them aside. Place the remaining strawberries and preserve in the bowl of a food processor, and process until puréed. Add the crème de Cassis.

2 At serving time, unmould the dessert on a rectangular platter. Sprinkle with a little sauce and decorate with the reserved sliced strawberries and crushed pistachios. To serve, divide the remaining sauce among six dessert plates, and top with a slice of the cold floating island.

Raspberry Granité

ESPECIALLY attractive when served in champagne glasses, this fresh-tasting sherbet is flavoured with raspberry brandy and garnished with mint sprigs. It makes a perfect finish to an elegant meal.

SERVES 4

350 g (12 oz) fresh raspberries or 1 packet (12 oz) frozen unsweetened raspberries
1 cup raspberry preserve
1 tablespoon fresh lemon juice
4 teaspoons raspberry brandy
4 sprigs fresh mint
Additional raspberries, for garnish

1 Place the raspberries and preserve in the bowl of a food processor and process until puréed. Strain through a fine strainer into a bowl (2 cups).

2 Add the lemon juice and mix. Place the bowl in the freezer for about 2½ hours. The mixture should be hard set but still soft enough in the centre so it can be mixed.

3 Transfer the purée to the bowl of a food processor and process for about 20 seconds. (It will 'whiten' slightly.) Return the puree to a bowl and place it back in the freezer for another 2½ –3 hours.

4 To serve, scoop into glass dishes and pour a teaspoon of the raspberry brandy over each serving. Decorate with a sprig of fresh mint and a few berries, if desired.

Buttermilk Strawberry Shortcake

HOME-MADE strawberry shortcake is a hit with just about everyone and this very easy recipe is no exception. The shortcakes are served with a garnish of sour cream, although yoghurt would make a good, lower-calorie substitute.

SERVES 4

550 g (1 1/4 lb) strawberries
1/2 cup strawberry jam

Shortcakes
1 cup plain flour
1 teaspoon baking powder
1/2 teaspoon baking soda
1 1/2 tablespoons sugar
3 tablespoons unsalted butter, softened
1/2 teaspoon granulated salt
1/3 cup buttermilk

1/2 cup sour cream
4 sprigs mint, for garnish

A WORD ABOUT SHORTCAKE

In this recipe, I use both baking powder and baking soda. Baking powder is made from a mixture of baking soda and cream of tartar (tartaric acid); I use baking soda in addition because of the sourness and acidity of the buttermilk. It is important that you mix the ingredients for the shortcakes lightly and quickly, combining them just enough so they hold together. Then, press them out on a tray with plastic wrap and cut them into squares, so there is no waste.

1 Rinse and hull the strawberries. Cut off abut 5 mm (1/4 in) from the stem end of each strawberry. (This part of the strawberry tends to be less sweet, especially if the strawberries are not completely ripe.) Reserve these trimmings for the sauce. You should have 2 cups of trimmings and 2 cups of trimmed berries.

2 Cut the trimmed strawberries into wedges and place them in a bowl. Transfer the trimmings to the bowl of a food processor. Add the jam to the strawberry trimmings and process until smooth. Pour the sauce over the strawberries, toss well and set aside in the refrigerator for at least 1 hour, or as long as 6 hours.

For shortcakes:
1 Pre-heat the oven to gas mark 8, 450°F (230°C). In a bowl, combine the flour, baking powder, soda, sugar and salt with the butter, mixing gently with a spoon for 30 seconds at most. (The mixture should not be completely smooth.) Add buttermilk and mix with a spoon just enough to combine the ingredients into a soft dough. Invert the dough onto a non-stick baking sheet and cover it with a piece of plastic wrap. Press on the dough until you have extended it to a thickness of about 1 cm (3/8 in), and then cut it into 6 cm (2 1/2 in) squares. Bake in the pre-heated oven for 10–12 minutes. Remove to a rack; cool.

2 At serving time, cut the shortcakes in half horizontally. Arrange bottoms on four dessert dishes and spoon strawberry mixture on top. Cover with the shortcake tops, and garnish each with sour cream and a sprig of mint. Serve.

Candied Orange Rind

THIS is an inexpensive treat, using only sugar and orange skins. The skins can be reserved in the refrigerator several days prior to candying. The candied rind will keep for several weeks or until needed, if stored in an airtight plastic container. It should be dry on the outside, but moist and chewy inside.

MAKES APPROXIMATELY 36 PIECES

2 large seedless navel oranges, 550 g (1¼ lb)

1⅓ cups sugar

1 Trim off both ends of the oranges and cut through their skin lengthwise in six equally-spaced places. With a sharp knife, remove the skin and pith underneath. If the cottony pith is very thick, remove some of it from the skin, holding your knife horizontally. The rind should not be much thicker than 1.5 mm (1/16 in; if thicker, it will take longer to cook.

2 If you have a vegetable peeler that cuts deeply, use it to remove 1.5mm (1/16 in) strips from the skin. Pile up the skin sections, and cut them into strips about (½ in) wide. You should have about 36 strips.

3 Place the strips in a saucepan, cover with 6 cups of cold tap water, and bring to the boil. Boil for 5 seconds, drain, and rinse under cool tap water. Return the strips to the washed pan with 1 cup of the sugar, and add 6 cups of cold tap water. Bring to the boil, and boil over a high heat for about 1 hour, until the rind is almost transparent and the syrup is just beginning to darken and become like caramel. Remove from the heat.

4 Spread the remaining ⅓ cup sugar on a baking sheet. With a fork, transfer the orange peel strips to the tray and press them into the sugar to coat on all sides. Arrange on a plate and allow to dry for 1 hour, then transfer to an airtight container for use as needed.

BLANCHING THE RIND

Be sure to blanch the rind well and then wash it before placing it back in the saucepan to cook in the sugar – it will be too bitter otherwise. Make sure that the pan has been cleaned before the washed rind goes back in!

Postscripts

Information About Nutrition
Techniques and Equipment
Vitamins and Minerals
Protein
Fibre
Complex Carbohydrates
Calories
Cholesterol
Fats and Fat Substitutes
Sugars
Salt and Sodium
Vegetables
Grains
Oils
Nutritional Charts
Index

Nutrition

CHANGING NUTRITIONAL EMPHASIS IN THE 1990S

To me, modern cuisine is really common-sense cuisine. Today's menus should consist of foods that are tasty and beautiful, as well as including a variety of foods that help to maintain healthy weight. They should be low in saturated fats and cholesterol, contain plenty of vegetables, fruits and grain products, and include sugars, salt and alcohol in moderation.

TECHNIQUES AND EQUIPMENT

I have found that using certain techniques and equipment in the kitchen can enhance the nutritional value of our foods. For instance, fats are the most calorie-laden food that we eat. With few exceptions, any reduction in our fat intake will improve our diets.

One excellent way to cut down on the use of fats in cooking is to use non-stick pans. The amount of fat that is used to saute in non-stick pans is less than half of what might be used in an untreated pan. I like to use non-stick pans with a permanent finish when I sauté and fry.

Grilling is also a great way to enhance the flavour of foods, and cook them without the addition of extra fats or salt.

There is great diversity in the types of grilling units available today. When I grill or barbecue, I like to use natural wood chips such as apple wood, olive wood or cherry wood for their delicious smoky flavour and ability to produce high heat. I often use wood charcoal because it is pre-cooked so it turns to hot coal more quickly. Charcoal briquettes are petroleum based and should be reduced to a grey-ash colour before cooking. This reduces the tar flavour that can be picked up from them.

VITAMINS AND MINERALS

For years, we have been concerned about the level of vitamins and minerals in our diets. Modern cooking has given us some new insight into this old subject.

We now know that the old way of cooking vegetables, which was to blanch them in large pots of boiling water and then refresh them in cold water before seasoning, resulted in the loss of essential vitamins and minerals. I recommend cooking vegetables in a small amount of boiling water just until the water disappears, thus retaining the maximum amount of vitamins and minerals.

Iron is a particular concern for many people, especially women. Many of my recipes, such as *Moules Maison* (page 57), *Clam Croquettes* (page 45), and *Beans and Escarole* (page 35), are high in iron.

PROTEIN

Red meat, long maligned as a high fat protein source has moved into the 1990s as a much lighter main course item. Now that livestock is being raised to produce leaner meat, we can get our iron and protein from these red meat sources without worrying about fat intake. By trimming the meat properly before cooking, and by serving smaller portions, red meat is part of a healthy gourmet diet.

FIBRE

Today, experts recommend a diet high in fibre to help reduce cholesterol. For you and me, that means approximately 25–30mg of fibre per day. Luckily, water soluble dietary fibre is contained in some delicious packages. Fibre is a part of plant foods. It is found in abundance in whole grain bread and cereals, vegetables, fresh and dried fruits and vegetables, or peas and beans like those found in the *Cauliflower in Spring Onion Sauce* (page 95), *Figs Villamora* (page 132), and *Quinoa with Sunflower Seeds* (page 75).

COMPLEX CARBOHYDRATES

Complex carbohydrates, which give us long lasting energy by slowly converting to sugars during digestion, do not necessarily need to be combined with high fat foods to be delicious. Complex carbohydrates are found in many of the foods which also happen to be rich in fibre, vitamins and minerals such as whole grain breads, cereals, pastas, rice, beans and potatoes.

CALORIES

Reducing calories does not necessarily mean eating tiny portions of trendy food. There are many hearty, filling dishes that you can prepare and consume knowing that they are very low in calories. I have included some of these dishes in *Today's Gourmet*. They are *Grilled Chicken with Cabbage Anchoïade* (page 69), *Poule au Pot* (page 70), *Sautéed Scallops with Mangetouts* (page 52), and *Salmon Pojarski* (page 60).

I have suggested several dessert recipes that are quite low in calories, too. While a typical portion of dessert often contains as many as 500 calories, the following desserts are much lighter and contain about one-third of the calories: *Pistachio Floating Island with Blackcurrant Sauce* (page 142), *Raspberry Granité* (page 143), and *Chocolate and Fruit Nut Cups* (page 127).

During the holidays, we all tend to consume a few extra calories that we might not eat during the rest of the year so I have suggested a holiday menu which contains approximately one-half of the calories of a normal holiday feast. The menu features *Sautéed Scallops with Mangetouts* (page 52), *Roasted Turkey with Mushroom Stuffing* (page 76), *Carrot Purée with Ginger* (page 98). *Chocolate Mint Truffles* (page 128), and *Candied Orange Rind* (page 146).

CHOLESTEROL

Various heart associations recommend that we consume 300mg or less of cholesterol per day. In most instances, I use oils instead of butter to cut down on cholesterol. In addition, I have created breakfast recipes which minimize the number of egg yolks that an individual consumes.

FATS AND FAT SUBSTITUTES

Experts believe that a healthy diet is one where no more than 30 per cent of the daily calories consumed are derived from the intake of fat. To achieve this percentage, I sometimes make low-fat substitutions in my recipes. For example, non-fat or low-fat yoghurt may be substituted for sour cream.

Some fats have been proven beneficial. Salmon, although it is a fatty fish, contains what is now described by experts as 'heart-healthy fats' or Omega 3s. These Omega 3s help keep blood from getting sticky and forming clots which lead to heart attacks. Fatty fishes have also been known to lower the fats in blood (called triglycerides). Because of these benefits, health experts are urging us to eat more fish, up to 6.75kg (15lb) per year.

SUGARS

It is important to remember to use moderation when consuming refined sugar. Refined sugar can lead to tooth decay, and when combined with fat, can be tremendously calorific. But, who can resist sweet treats during the holidays? For this reason, I included recipes for *Chocolate Mint Truffles* (page 128) and *Chocolate and Fruit Nut Cups* (page 127). A small bit of richness can help you to feel satisifed without overdoing it.

We often eat too much sugar for breakfast, too. Why not eat a savoury, high-protein breakfast suggested in the menu on page 21?

SALT AND SODIUM

I have some special tips to cut down on salt. Because I like highly seasoned foods, I use a variety of seasonings as salt substitutes. Tabasco sauce, plenty of fresh herbs and strongly flavoured spices are excellent substitutes.

The key to reducing the amount of salt used in cooking is to bring out the natural flavour in the food itself. For example, if you crystallize the juices on the outside of meat before cooking it, you can bring out the flavour without adding salt. Another way to enhance flavour is to use citrus fruits such as lemon or lime, or any number of the fresh herbs and spices available today. And don't forget about flavour-enhancing cooking techniques, such as grilling or steaming.

VEGETABLES

Vegetables are the most important kind of food to emphasize in our diets. They are naturally low in calories, and high in fibre, vitamins and minerals. Whenever possible, I buy organic fruits and vegetables for their fantastic flavour and guaranteed wholesomeness. My friend, Alice Waters, of *Chez Panisse* Restaurant, says that by purchasing organic fruits and vegetables, we support the people who work to preserve and enhance our farmland.

When I was young, my mother was an organic gardener, and she didn't even know it! But this was in a time when organic farming was not a speciality it was a way of life.

GRAINS

Adding whole grains to your diet is a great way to add protein, fibre and complex carbohydrates. I often use traditional grains like Cream of Wheat (the centre of the wheat berry) and oats in non-traditional ways. My *Chicken and Spinach Velouté* (page 28) and *Oatmeal Leek Soup* (page 32) are good examples. Also I recommend using grains that are now becoming popular like quinoa, featured with grilled quail on page 132.

OILS

In today's supermarket, you will find a vast selection of oils. I think that it is important to understand the nature of oils, in order to know which one to choose. For instance, some oils are lower in saturated fat than others, some are more strongly flavoured, and some may even burn at a relatively low temperature, giving off a bad smell and flavour.

At room temperature, all oils are liquid fat. Some oils, like palm oil, are very high in saturated fat and therefore can boost the level of blood cholesterol. In much of my cooking, I try to use the oil that is lowest in saturated fat – corn or rapeseed oil.

Extra virgin oil is usually dark, with a rich olive flavour. The colour and flavour is the result of olive solids that are present in the oil. Extra virgin olive oil is so named because it has been removed from the olives by mechanical pressing, from the sheer weight of the olives. No heat or chemical processes are used to extract this oil. These olive solids which impart flavour and colour burn at fairly low temperatures, so extra virgin olive oil is best used for salads and marinades.

The best oils for use in sautéeing are flavourless safflower, corn, or for a mild flavour groundnut oil. These oils are ideal for sautéeing because they can withstand high temperatures without burning.

	Calories	Protein(gm)	Carbohydrates(gm)	Saturated Fat(gm)	Cholesterol(mg)	Sodium(mg)
Almond Cake with Mango Coulis	254	6	30	2	67	29
Asparagus in Mustard Sauce	82	2	3	.51	0	387
Baked Apple Tart	263	2	41	6	27	3
Baked Apricots with Almonds	101	2	18	1	4	7
Baked Bananas in Lemon and Rum Sauce	217	2	52	.05	0	5
Baked Pears with Figs	248	2	57	2	8	8
Beans and Escarole	313	18	40	2	12	731
Beef Carpaccio	269	19	3	5	47	485
Blueberries with Brown Sugar	110	2	25	.28	2	28
Braised Pork Cocotte	248	27	11	3	72	277
Braised Sour Cabbage	178	3	38	1	4	443
Braised Stuffed Artichokes	300	5	25	3	.54	578
Broccoli Piquante	90	3	6	.96	0	167
Brown Rice Chicken Fricassee	324	16	46	9	54	828
Buttermilk Bread	404	13	67	5	23	420
Figs in Spicy Port Sauce	250	4	60	.54	2	38
Candied Orange Rind	90	.11	23	0	0	0
Caramelized Apple Timbales	168	.36	37	2	8	2
Carotte Ciboulette	73	1	11	2	8	477
Cauliflower in Spring Onion Sauce	112	2	5	1	.08	154
Cherry Bread Pudding	241	5	42	2	8	85
Chicken and Seafood Paella	626	29	53	10	166	868
Chicken and Spinach Velouté	175	3	19	5	27	446
Chicken in Tarragon Sauce	215	28	5	4	107	377
Chicken Legs with Wine and Yams	433	43	32	3	155	462
Chicken Broth	40	48	5	0	0	1
Chocolate and Fruit Nut Cups	176	3	19	6	0	2

	Calories	Protein(gm)	Carbohydrates(gm)	Saturated Fat(gm)	Cholesterol(mg)	Sodium(mg)
Chocolate Mint Truffles	157	3	14	7	54	6
Chocolate Soufflé Cake with Raspberry-Rum Sauce	349	6	37	10	78	54
Clam Croquettes	282	9	9	3	24	340
Coffee Crème Caramel	122	6	16	2	66	75
Corn and Pepper Sauté	129	3	17	4	16	149
Cornmeal au Gruyère	148	6	17	3	16	323
Couscous of Lobster	568	33	59	3	82	782
Crab Cakes with Avocado Sauce	325	13	7	4	63	522
Crêpes Soufflés with Grapefruit Sauce	206	6	27	2	41	118
Croque Monsieur	317	17	20	7	47	656
Curried Bulgar with Currants	190	5	34	.53	0	28
Figs Villamora	288	5	61	.67	0	11
Fresh Fruit with Minted Apricot Fondue	286	4	85	1	0	13
French Fries	278	4	36	2	0	12
Fricassee Claudine	385	18	44	8	66	177
Garlic Soup	289	6	36	3	9	651
Grapes and Raisins in Lime Biscuit Cone	134	2	24	1	5	11
Gratin of Spring Onions	189	11	31	3	14	239
Grilled Chicken with Cabbage Anchoïade	520	57	11	4	135	1228
Grilled Lamb Chops with Savory	171	19	.45	3	61	328
Grilled Leg of Lamb	279	37	8	4	114	346
Grilled Quail with Quinoa	178	17	2	3	00	46
Hazelnut Parfait with Candied Violets	369	5	10	13	68	20
Hot Prawns on Spinach	236	221	4	.2	140	328
Irish Lamb Stew	271	26	27	4	74	502
James Beard's Onion Sandwiches	279	4	25	3	13	484

	Calories	Protein(gm)	Carbohydrates(gm)	Saturated Fat(gm)	Cholesterol(mg)	Sodium(mg)
Jam Sandwiches	222	2	28	3	56	44
Leeks with Tomato and Olive Oil	272	7	41	2	0	470
Moules Maison	295	19	18	2	37	680
Mushroom Omelette	280	10	13	14	290	282
Mushroom-stuffed Potato Pancakes	195	2	18	1	0	439
Mushroom Stuffing	161	3	22	.80	.49	277
Mussels Gratinée	336	18	19	11	130	711
Oatmeal Leek Soup	224	11	27	5	30	384
Oeuf Cocotte	165	8	14	3	220	262
Olive and Tomato Toasts	318	6	26	3	3	983
Oranges and Grapefruit Segments	136	2	35	.01	0	2
Oranges in Grand Marnier	127	.88	29	.03	0	.12
Pan Bagna	467	15	73	2	7	1575
Pasta and Courgettes	275	8	35	2	2	236
Pasta with Fresh Vegetable Sauce	343	10	42	16	44	632
Peas à la Française	161	5	20	.98	0	675
Pistachio Floating Island with Blackcurrant Sauce	196	5	35	.62	.85	47
Pommes Anglaises	127	3	28	0	0	12
Pommes Persillade	176	3	21	2	8	79
Potage de Légumes au Vermicelli	227	6	39	1	4	569
Potatoe Crêpes with Caviar	519	25	20	10	538	1256
Poule au Pot	501	45	58	4	121	1365
Poulet au Vin Rouge	421	47	21	3	144	708
Purée of Carrot with Ginger	136	2	16	1	2	473
Ragout of Rabbit	409	44	7	22	131	508
Raspberry Granité	277	1	68	1	0	11

	Calories	Protein(gm)	Carbohydrates(gm)	Saturated Fat(gm)	Cholesterol(mg)	Sodium(mg)
Red Snapper in Potato Jackets	381	32	20	19	52	491
Roasted Aubergine Sandwiches	514	16	60	25	22	402
Roasted Turkey	474	78	5	13	219	421
Salmon Pojarski	243	23	13	10	55	681
Salpicon of Pineapple	127	.52	25	.50	0	3
Saucisses an Chou on Lentils	449	26	27	27	65	997
Sautéed Aubergine Rolls	475	11	23	40	24	756
Sautéed Salmon on Greens	361	31	9	23	78	517
Sauteed Scallops with Mangetout	190	16	8	11	36	280
Smoked Pork Roast with Mustard-Honey Glaze	159	21	4	2	41	1047
Smoked Salmon and Cucumber Sandwiches	250	17	32	5	32	453
Smoked Salmon Mould	180	12	13	9	36	550
Spicy Beef Roast	238	31	1	31	87	219
Split Pea Soup with Crackling	373	21	49	11	13	754
Steamed Cod on Tapenade	359	29	9	24	65	1274
Steamed Chicory with Lemon Juice	55	2	6	3	8	148
Strawberry Buttermilk Shortcake	404	5	63	15	37	526
Tomato, Onion and Parsley Vinaigrette	133	4	9	19	10	188
Trout Sauté Terry	438	38	7	29	116	844
Tuna Tartare on Marinated Cucumbers	249	27	4	14	43	737
Turnips and Mashed Potatoes	151	3	22	6	15	304
Veal Chops with Mushrooms	305	30	6	18	120	404
Veal Roast with Artichokes	340	42	20	10	168	578
Wine Merchant Steak	382	44	7	18	117	689

Other cookery titles published by BBC Books include

Michael Barry's Food and Drink Cookbook
Sarah Brown's Vegetarian Kitchen
Antonio Carluccio's Passion for Pasta
A Taste of Japan *Leslie Downer*
Floyd's American Pie *Keith Floyd*
Floyd on Britain and Ireland *Keith Floyd*
Floyd on Fire *Keith Floyd*
Floyd on Fish *Keith Floyd*
Floyd on France *Keith Floyd*
Valentina Harris's Complete Italian Cookery Course
Valentina's Italian Regional Cookery *Valentina Harris*
Ken Hom's Chinese Cookery
Madhur Jaffrey's Far Eastern Cookery
Madhur Jaffrey's Indian Cookery
Mireille Johnston's French Cookery Course, Part 1
Mediterranean Cookery *Claudia Roden*
At Home with the Roux Brothers *Albert & Michel Roux*
Spain on a Plate *María José Sevilla*
Delia Smith's Christmas
Delia Smith's Complete Cookery Course
Delia Smith Complete Illustrated Cookery Course
Eating Out with Tovey *John Tovey*
Entertaining on a Plate *John Tovey*
Hot Chefs *Various*

Index